Table of Contents

What Is a Map?

Concept: Maps are necessary tools in today's world.

Objective: To help students understand why it is important to know how to read a map.

Vocabulary: map, explorer, satellite, cartographer, maze

Background Information:
- The earliest maps were often drawn in the dirt or sand. Their purpose was to help people find food and water.
- The oldest known map is a small clay tablet from Babylonia showing a man's estate. It was made in 2300 B.C.
- One of the oldest Egyptian maps shows a route from the Nile Valley to gold mines.
- Ancient maps were incomplete and showed the earth as a flat area.
- Explorers to North America drew maps to help guide themselves and others across the new land.
- At the present time, photographs taken from airplanes and satellites are a big help to cartographers. Computers also assist cartographers in many ways.

Teaching Suggestions

1. Introduce the concept of maps by asking students the following questions:
   a. Where have you seen maps?
   b. Who have you seen using a map?
   c. What kind of information do you think is on a map?
   d. Why would these people need a map? – truck driver, fireman, police officer, astronaut.

2. Tell students that the main purpose of a map is to help someone find his or her way. Ask students if they have ever worked a maze. Explain that finding the correct path in a maze and using a map are similar. Have students complete the activity page *Finding the Treasure*.

3. Ask students to explain the difference between a picture and a map. A picture shows what things look like. A map shows where things or places are located. Maps look as if they were drawn from the view of someone sitting in an airplane. Have the students complete the activity page *A Picture from Above*.

4. Some maps show where things are located in one area, such as a town. They can show how to get from one place to another and sometimes they even show how far one place is from another. Have the students complete the activity page *Going from Place to Place*.

Additional Activities

1. Have students each draw a maze which may be exchanged with other students during an extra ten minutes before lunch or at the end of the day.

2. Have students draw a map of their bedroom. They should pretend to sit on the ceiling and draw the things they see on the floor.

3. Take the students outside and have them each draw a map of the playground or a map of the school grounds including the building, play area, and parking area.

Finding the Treasure

Name _____

Find the correct path through the maze. Use your pencil to draw a line from "Start" to "Finish."

Next draw your own maze on another sheet of paper.

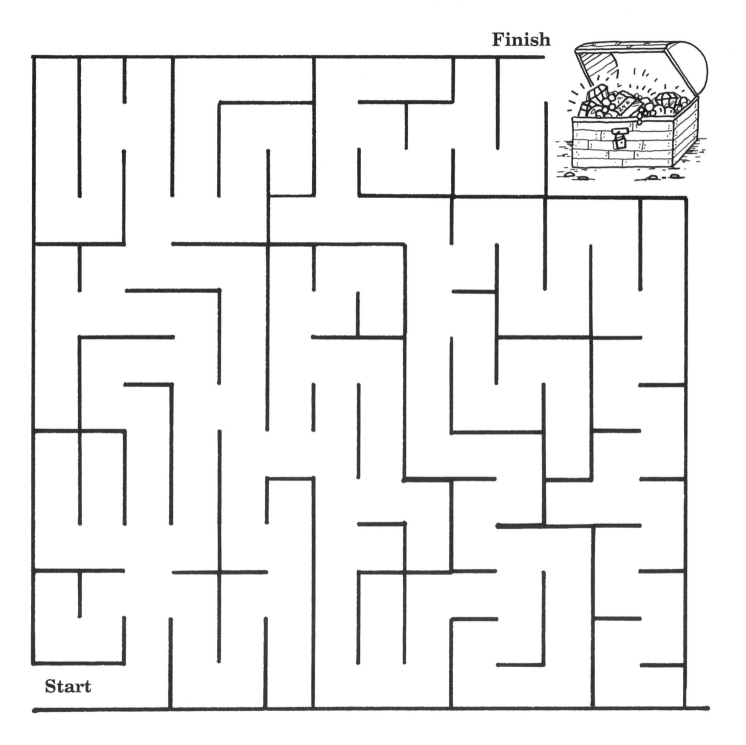

A Picture from Above

Name _____

A map looks like a picture someone drew looking down from the sky. Maps show you where things are.

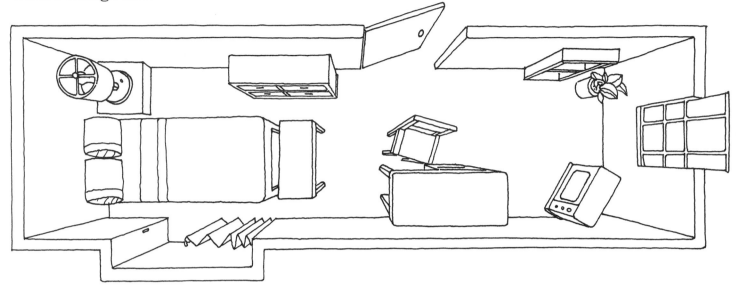

Circle the word which correctly completes each statement.

1. The TV is near the . . .   a. door   b. window   c. bed
2. The dresser is near the . . .   a. window   b. door   c. TV
3. Next to the bed is a . . .   a. TV   b. window   c. table
4. The bench is at the end of the . . . a. bed   b. bookshelf   c. closet
5. The plant is by the . . .   a. dresser   b. bed   c. window
6. The bookshelf is next to the . . . a. bed   b. closet   c. door
7. The lamp is on the . . .   a. table   b. TV   c. dresser

Follow these directions.

1. Draw a red circle around the TV.
2. Place a black **X** on the desk.
3. Draw an oval rug in front of the bench using a color of your choice.
4. Draw a stuffed animal in the center of the bed.

Fill in these blanks with the correct word.

1. Between the closet and TV is a _____ .
2. The window is between the _____ and the TV.
3. When you walk in the door, the _____ is to your right.
4. There is _____ lamp(s) in the room.

Going from Place to Place

Name _____

Some maps show you where places are located in a town.

Britt City

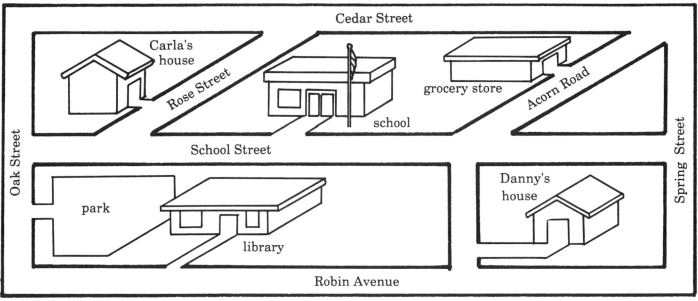

Circle the word that tells which is *closest* to Danny's house.

1. Carla's house   OR   The Library
2. Robin Avenue   OR   Oak Street
3. The Park   OR   The Grocery Store
4. Spring Street   OR   Cedar Street

Circle the word that tells which is *farthest* from Carla's house.

1. Spring Street   OR   Rose Street
2. The Park   OR   Danny's house
3. School   OR   The Library
4. Oak Street   OR   Acorn Road

Add the following items to the map of Britt City.

1. Draw a flower garden on the corner of Spring Street and Robin Avenue.
2. Draw a swimming pool behind Carla's house.
3. Draw a baseball or football field behind the school.
4. Draw a car in front of Carla's house.
5. Draw a school bus on School Street.
6. Use a red crayon to draw the shortest path from Carla's house to Danny's.

Continents and Oceans

Concept: The surface of the earth is made up of large land masses called continents and large bodies of water called oceans.

Objective: To show that the surface of the earth is composed of continents and oceans.

Vocabulary: continent, ocean, globe, hemisphere, Western Hemisphere, Eastern Hemisphere, Northern Hemisphere, Southern Hemisphere

Background Information:
- The surface of the earth is divided into land and water. The majority, about 70%, of the surface is water. These large bodies of water are oceans: the Pacific (about 63,800,000 square miles), the Atlantic (about 31,530,000 square miles), the Indian (about 28,356,000 square miles), and the Arctic (about 3,662,000 square miles).
- The salt water found in the oceans is not drinkable.
- The large land masses, called continents, comprise approximately 30% of the earth's surface. The seven continents are Asia (17,000,000 square miles), Africa (11,700,000 square miles), North America (9,400,000 square miles), South America (6,900,000 square miles), Antarctica (5,100,000 square miles), Europe (4,063,000 square miles), and Australia (2,966,000 square miles).

Teaching Suggestions

1. Use a globe to introduce the terms *continent* and *ocean*. Explain that the globe is round like the earth. Have the students come to your desk in groups of five or six for a closer look at the globe and its features. Point out the seven continents and four oceans. After all students have had a close-up view, ask the class if there is more land or more water on the globe. Explain to the students that the earth is about 70% water and about 30% land.

2. Next use a large map of the earth to again point out the seven continents. Write the names on the board: North America, South America, Africa, Asia, Europe, Antarctica, and Australia.

3. Remind the students that most of the earth's surface is composed of water. Point out the four large oceans on a map: Atlantic, Pacific, Indian, and Arctic. Write these names on the board. Explain to the class that the oceans are composed of salt water. At this time, have the students complete the activity page *Land and Water*.

4. Show the students on a large map that you must fly or take a ship to get from one continent to most other continents. This is due to the large oceans which surround most continents. Use the activity page *Let's Travel the Earth* at this time.

5. Before passing out the activity page *Locating the Continents and Oceans,* introduce the word *hemisphere* to the students. Talk about the different ways the world can be divided: Northern and Southern Hemispheres or Eastern and Western Hemispheres. The concept of a hemisphere will be much easier for the students to understand if you explain with large maps of the world. The best type of map would be a hemisphere map. Also, some globes are designed to be taken apart to demonstrate the hemispheres. If you do not have the appropriate maps or globes in your classroom, check with your media specialist and/or librarian. They often have these types of maps or globes.

Additional Activities

1. Make one copy of the map used on the activity page *Let's Travel the Earth*. Draw lines on it to resemble a jigsaw puzzle. Run off copies for each student. Have the students color the puzzle map and then cut it out. They now have a puzzle to use in their spare time. You may want to provide each student with an envelope for their puzzle pieces.

2. Have the students make a chart of the following information for all seven continents and four oceans: name of each, its area in square miles, and the population of each continent. This information can be found in an atlas or encyclopedia. You may wish to have the students work in pairs.

Land and Water

Name _____

Use the map below plus a wall map to do this activity.

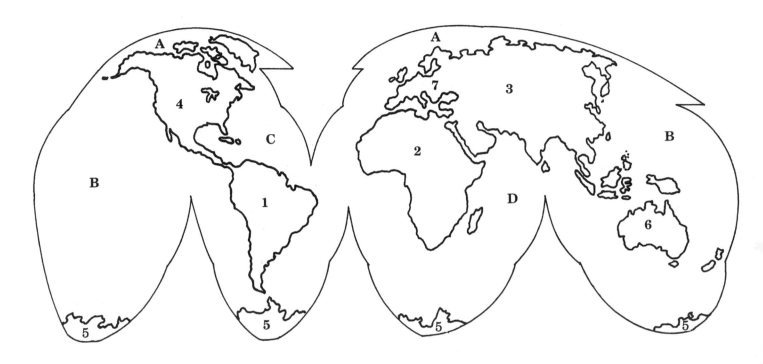

Write the name of each continent in the correct blank.

1. _____   5. _____
2. _____   6. _____
3. _____   7. _____
4. _____

Write the name of each ocean in the correct blank.

A. _____   C. _____
B. _____   D. _____

Use crayons or markers to follow these directions.

1. Color Australia green.   5. Color North America red.
2. Color Europe yellow.   6. Color South America brown.
3. Color Africa orange.   7. Color Asia purple.
4. Color Antarctica blue.

Let's Travel the Earth

Name _____

Use the map on page 9 to answer the questions below.

Circle the word that correctly completes each statement.

1. If you sail from North America to Antarctica, you will be on the . . .

Arctic Ocean   Atlantic Ocean   Indian Ocean

2. If you fly from Africa to Australia, you will fly over the . . . .

Indian Ocean   Pacific Ocean   Atlantic Ocean

3. To sail from Europe to South America, you will sail on the . . .

Pacific Ocean   Arctic Ocean   Atlantic Ocean

4. To sail from North America to Europe, you will sail on the . . .

Indian Ocean   Atlantic Ocean   Pacific Ocean

5. To travel from Europe to Asia, you must cross . . .

the Pacific Ocean   the Indian Ocean   land

Fill in the blanks with the correct word.

1. The continent above South America is _____

2. The ocean directly below Asia is the _____

3. The ocean directly above Asia is the _____

4. The continent directly below Europe is _____

5. The continent directly below Australia is _____

Use a crayon or marker to follow these directions.

1. Draw a red line from North America to Africa.
2. Draw a green line from Asia to Antarctica.
3. Draw an orange line from Australia to Africa.
4. Draw a black line from Europe to South America.
5. Circle the names of all four oceans with blue.
6. Color North America green.
7. Draw a black dotted line (▬ ▬ ▬ ▬ ▬) around South America.

Let's Travel the Earth
(Continued)

Name _____

Use with page 8.

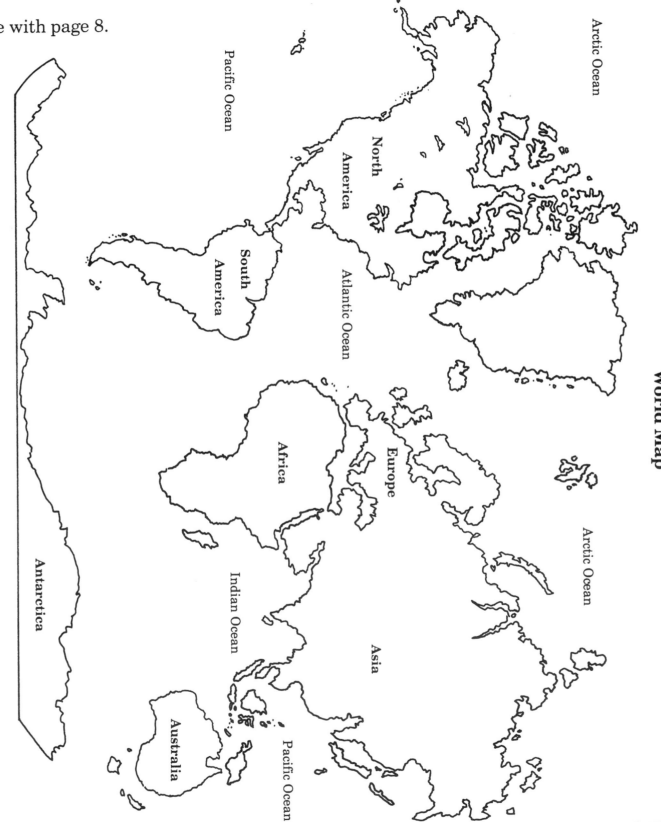

World Map

Arctic Ocean

Pacific Ocean

North America

Atlantic Ocean

South America

Africa

Europe

Arctic Ocean

Antarctica

Indian Ocean

Asia

Australia

Pacific Ocean

Locating the Continents and Oceans

Name _____

Use these maps plus wall maps to complete this page and the next. Note: Some continents belong to more than one hemisphere.

Eastern Hemisphere

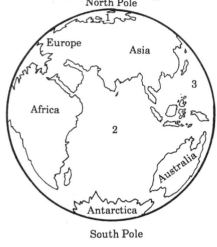

Western Hemisphere

Northern Hemisphere

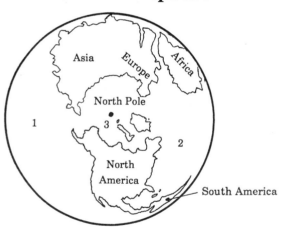

Southern Hemisphere

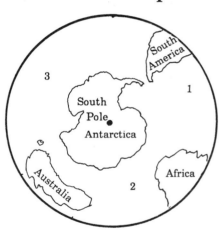

1. Which continent is found in both the Eastern and Western Hemispheres?

_____

2. Which map does not show any part of Antarctica?

_____

3. Which hemisphere does not include any part of Africa?

_____

4. Color the continent located entirely in the Western and Northern Hemispheres red.

5. Color the continent located entirely in the Eastern and Southern Hemispheres blue.

Locating the Continents and Oceans (Continued)

Name _____

Use with page 10. Fill in the blanks.

Continents in Eastern Hemisphere

_____

_____

_____

_____

Continents in Western Hemisphere

_____

_____

_____

Continents in Northern Hemisphere

_____

_____

_____

_____

Continents in Southern Hemisphere

_____

_____

_____

Oceans in Eastern Hemisphere

1. _____

2. _____

3. _____

Oceans in Western Hemisphere

1. _____

2. _____

3. _____

Oceans in Northern Hemisphere

1. _____

2. _____

3. _____

Oceans in Southern Hemisphere

1. _____

2. _____

3. _____

Land and Water Formations

Concept: The surface of the earth is covered with land and water formations created by nature.

Objective: To describe the various land and water formations on the earth's surface.

Vocabulary: strait, valley, river, plateau, peninsula, mountain, bay, cape, isthmus, island, lake, delta, volcano, tributary

Background Information:
- The surface of the earth is covered by many types of land and water formations. The passage of time and the forces of nature (ice, wind, and water) formed these physical features.
- As water flows across land, it picks up soil and carries it away. Over a long period of time, water carries so much soil away that valleys and canyons are formed. Wind also carries soil away. During a severe dry period (drought), wind carries away the top soil and by doing so changes the face of the earth.
- Some mountains and islands were created by volcanic eruption. Others were formed by the folding or breaking movements which occur within the earth's crust.
- Earthquakes have changed the paths of rivers. They have also created new lakes. Long ago, the slow movement of glaciers across the earth changed the earth's surface.
- Despite man's technology, the forces of nature cannot be controlled, and the earth's surface continues to change.

Teaching Suggestions

1. One way to introduce this topic is by using filmstrips and films. *National Geographic* has some especially good films on the forces of nature. There is also a recent filmstrip detailing the eruption of Mt. Saint Helens that should be of interest to students.

2. The students will need a large map of the United States to complete the activity pages in this unit.

3. You may wish to use activity page *Created by Nature* as a spelling or language arts lesson. Have the students spell the terms and then use them in a sentence.

4. Activity page *Can You Identify Nature's Creations?* shows a map of an imaginary planet. This activity may be more difficult than it appears. You could place a similar drawing on the board as an example before using the activity page and have the students identify the features first as a class.

5. The activity page *Are You a Cartographer?* will allow you to easily check each student's understanding. It should also be fun for the students.

Additional Activities

1. If you live in an area with easy access to some of the natural features described in this unit, a field trip would be fun. We all understand better when we can see, hear, and touch.

2. Ask someone from your state Geological Society to speak to your class about land and water formations.

Created by Nature

Name _____

Fill in each blank with the number of the land or water formation described.

1. strait   2. valley   3. river   4. plateau   5. peninsula   6. mountain

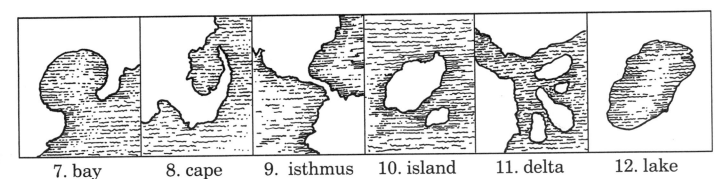

7. bay   8. cape   9. isthmus   10. island   11. delta   12. lake

_____ Part of a sea or lake which reaches into the land along the shore.
_____ Narrow landform connecting two larger pieces of land.
_____ A mass of mud and silt deposited by a river at its mouth.
_____ Land extending into the sea beyond the rest of the shoreline.
_____ Body of water encircled by land.
_____ Land mass completely surrounded by water.
_____ Land jutting from mainland and surrounded by water on three sides.
_____ Narrow channel of water connecting two larger bodies of water.
_____ Stream of water which flows over land and empties into another body of water.
_____ Broad, flat region, higher than its surroundings on at least one side.
_____ High, rocky land usually with steep sides.
_____ Lowland between hills or mountains.

Use a map of the United States to complete these.

1. Name one large mountain range found in the United States. _____

2. Name one of the fifty states which is a peninsula. _____

3. Name the state which is composed of islands. _____

4. Name the Great Lakes. _____

Can You Identify Nature's Creations?

Name _____

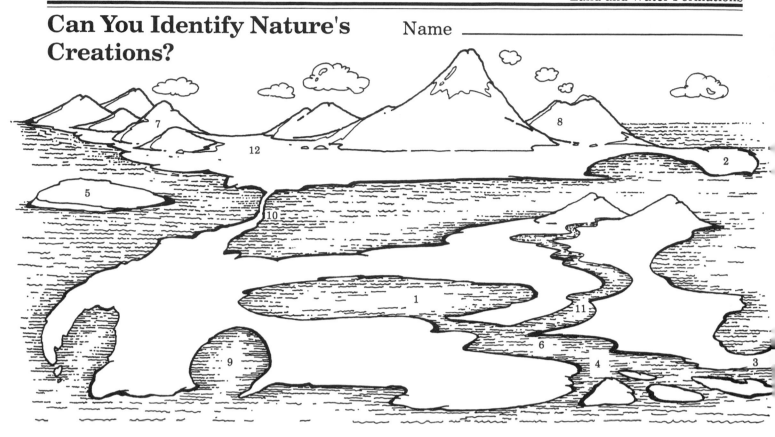

The formations on this map are numbered. Write each number next to the correct description below.

_____ A *cape* is land extending into the sea beyond the rest of the shoreline.

_____ A *delta* is a mass of mud and silt deposited by a river at its mouth.

_____ An *isthmus* is a narrow strip of land joining two large land areas.

_____ A *valley* is the low land between hills or mountains.

_____ A *river* is a stream of water flowing over land toward another body of water.

_____ A *peninsula* is a piece of land almost surrounded by water.

_____ A *tributary* is a stream that flows into a larger river.

_____ A *mountain* is a very high hill.

_____ A *bay* is part of an ocean or lake extending into land.

_____ A *lake* is a body of water surrounded by land.

_____ An *island* is a small body of land surrounded by water.

_____ A *volcano* is an opening in the earth that shoots out lava, rock, gases and ashes from time to time.

Follow these directions to complete the map.

1. Color the valley green.
2. Color the volcano red.
3. Add three houses below the lake.
4. Add three trees to the island.
5. Draw a sailboat on the lake.
6. Draw two hotels on the peninsula.

Are You a Cartographer?

Name _____

Draw a map which shows the land and water formations listed below. Since you are the cartographer, you should name each one.

A. Two mountain ranges
B. One volcano
C. Two lakes
D. Two peninsulas

E. Three islands
F. One isthmus
G. One river
H. One bay

Boundaries

Concept: A boundary is designed to set limits.

Objective: To show how boundaries are designed to set limits, whether natural or man-made.

Vocabulary: boundary, survey, isthmus, Western Hemisphere, mountains, sea

Background Information:
- Nature provided water, mountains, and an isthmus as boundaries which separate the seven continents.
- Five of the continents – North America, South America, Europe, Asia, and Africa – are subdivided into countries.
- The majority of boundaries between countries were set by people, usually at the end of a war.
- The boundaries between countries in Europe have been ever-changing in this century. World Wars I and II both changed the size and shape of European countries.
- The boundaries of the United States were not finalized until this century.

Teaching Suggestions

1. On a large map of the world, show the students the natural boundaries found between the continents. First point out the *oceans;* then show the location of the *Isthmus of Panama,* which separates North America and South America; the *Mediterranean Sea,* between Europe and Africa; and the *Ural Mountains,* between Europe and Asia. Write the names of all of the continents and natural boundaries on the board to help the students complete the activity page *What Divides the Land and Water?* This activity requires the students to label the continents and their boundaries.

2. Use a large map of the Western Hemisphere to explain the boundaries found within those continents. Point out the different types of borders separating the countries of North and South America. For example, surveyors plotted most of the border between Canada and the United States; the Rio Grande River divides the United States and Mexico; the Andes Mountains divide Chile and Argentina. Hand out the activity page *What Is Where in North and South America?*

3. The large countries of North America are subdivided into smaller parts of land. Use a large map of the United States to show boundaries between the states. Many of these boundaries were drawn by people and a few evolved from natural features: Red River between Texas and Oklahoma; Mississippi River between Missouri and Illinois; Sierra Nevada Mountains between California and Nevada. Pass out the activity page *Dividing the States.*

Additional Activities

1. Divide the class into groups of three or four students. Ask them to think of as many things as they can which set limits or establish boundaries. Examples: mountains, water, fence, parents, age, strength, etc. Have them let their imaginations flow. As long as they can explain their reasons for a particular answer, it should be acceptable. Set a time limit of one minute for the first list. Share all answers with the class. Give them another minute to double the number on their list *without* duplicating previously given answers.

2. Give pairs of students a political map of the United States. Ask them to reduce the number of states from 50 to 25 by redrawing the boundaries.

3. Other fun ways to help your students learn states and boundaries are by making use of various educational games and puzzles available at your local teachers' store.

What Divides the Land and Water?

Name _____

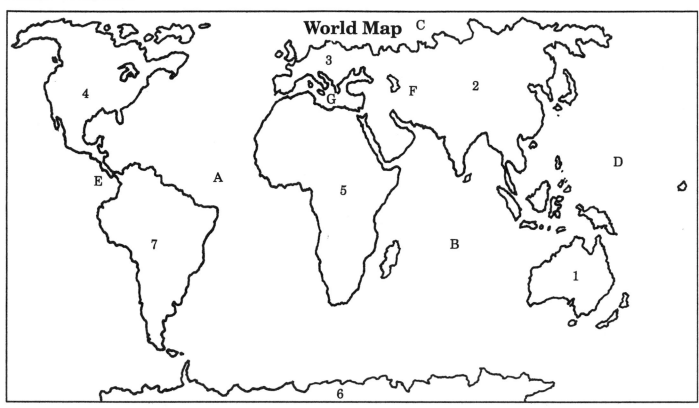

Write the names of the continents in the blanks.

1. _____   5. _____
2. _____   6. _____
3. _____   7. _____
4. _____

Write the names of the natural boundaries between the continents.

A. _____   E. _____

B. _____   F. _____

C. _____   G. _____

D. _____

Follow these directions to finish the map.

• Draw three stars in North America.
• Draw two arrows in South America.
• Draw a panda in Asia.
• Draw five diamonds in Africa.

What Is Where In North and South America

Name _____

North and South America

Follow these directions to complete the map. You may also use a political map of North and South America.

1. Outline Canada in red.
2. Outline the United States in black. (Do not forget Alaska and Hawaii.)
3. Outline Mexico in orange.
4. Outline Brazil in brown.
5. Outline Chile in red.
6. Outline Argentina in orange.
7. Outline Paraguay in yellow.
8. Outline Colombia in black.
9. Outline Bolivia in red.
10. Color Peru yellow.
11. Color Ecuador orange.
12. Color Uruguay brown.
13. Color Venezuela purple.
14. Color Guyana pink.
15. Color Suriname orange.
16. Color French Guiana yellow.
17. Color the Gulf of Mexico green.
18. Color the Arctic Ocean blue.
19. Color the Pacific Ocean grey.
20. Color the Atlantic Ocean purple.

Dividing the States

Name _____

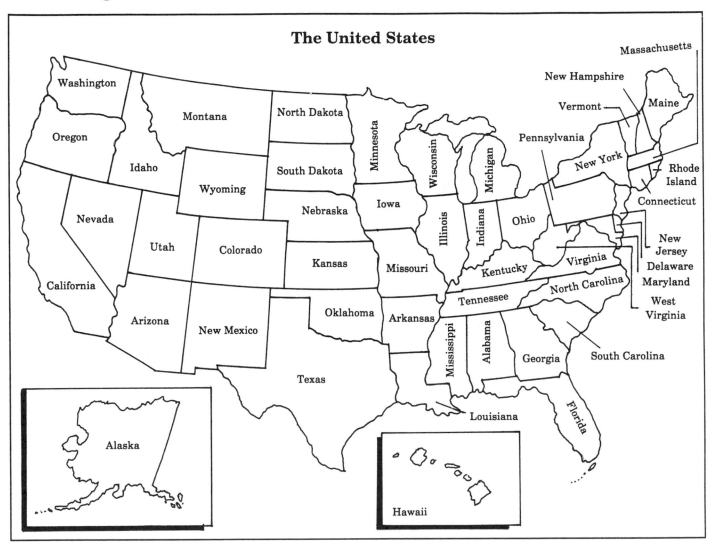

The United States

1. Name the four states which border Alabama. _____

   _____

   _____

2. Name the only state which borders Maine. _____

3. Name the three states which border California. _____

   _____

4. Name the state between Arizona and Texas. _____

5. Outline your home state in red.

6. Outline the states which form the boundaries of your state in blue.

7. Color all the states you have visited yellow.

8. Color the state you would like to visit green.

Cardinal Directions

Concept: Cardinal directions on a map help people locate things or places.

Objective: To show that the four cardinal directions on a map are north, south, east, and west.

Vocabulary: compass rose, direction, cardinal direction, equator, prime meridian

Background Information:
- Being able to read a map requires an understanding of map language.
- Map language begins with understanding the word *direction*, which means *which way*.
- The equator is an imaginary line which divides the earth into the north and south. All places above the equator are north and all places below the equator are south.
- The prime meridian is another imaginary line which divides the earth into east and west. Places to the right of the prime meridian are east and places to the left are west.

Teaching Suggestions

1. Use a globe to show the students the location of both the North and South Poles. Then show them again on a map. Also point out the equator and prime meridian. Remind the students that the equator and prime meridian are imaginary lines that do not exist physically.

2. Draw a compass rose on the board. Explain that a compass rose shows the location of directions on most maps they will use. At this stage you may wish to use the terms *up, down, left,* and *right* to help the students understand the four cardinal directions. It is especially important that they know *north* is almost always *up* on a map. Sometimes it is helpful to take them outside and have them face each of the four directions. They may also remember a little better if you remind them that the sun always rises in the east and sets in the west. The activity page *Connect-A-Dot* is a direction map.

3. After the students complete activity page *Connect-A-Dot,* you may want to use a large map of the United States for some oral repetition on cardinal directions. For instance, ask them to tell you which state is north, south, east, or west of other states. The activity pages *Is It North, South, East, or West?* and *Finding Your Way Around Town* will give students additional practice in the use of cardinal directions.

Additional Activities

1. Give the students a blank sheet of paper. Read the following: (A) Draw a house in the middle of the page; (B) Make a driveway south of the house; (C) Draw a flower garden east of the house; (D) Draw three trees west of the house; (E) Draw the sun north of the house; (F) Draw some birds in flight west of the sun; (G) Draw a birdbath south of the flower garden; (H) Draw a swing set west of the trees; (I) Draw a bicycle east of the driveway.

2. Have the students construct their own connect-a-dot direction map for other students to complete. You will need to provide them with a connect-a-dot sheet.

3. Run off enough blank bingo cards for each student. Have them write the names of the cardinal directions in the spaces on the cards. (You may wish to make the cards five spaces across and four spaces down.) Make up a list of questions about things in your classroom or school. After making sure they know where the directions are located, ask them the questions. Examples of questions are: Which direction is the teacher's desk from the door? Which direction is the filing cabinet from the red bookcase? Which direction is the floor from the ceiling? Which direction is Susie from the windows? Which direction is Johnny from Brett? Is Brice's desk north, south, east, or west of the chalkboard?

Connect – A – Dot

Name _____

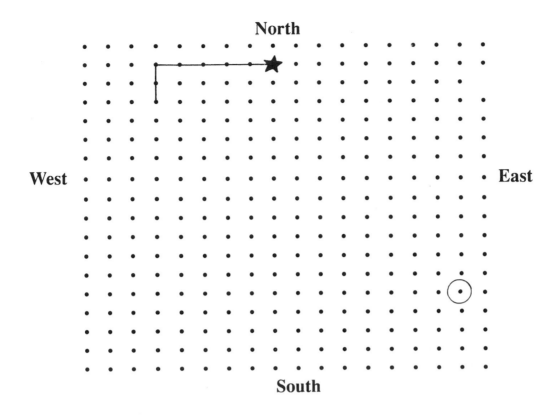

North

West   East

South

Follow these directions to complete a drawing. Begin at the star. The first two steps are done for you.

Draw a straight line . . .

1. Five spaces west.
2. Two spaces south.
3. Four spaces east.
4. Nine spaces south.
5. Two spaces east.

6. Nine spaces north.
7. Four spaces east.
8. Two spaces north.
9. Five spaces west.

What letter did you draw? _____

Begin at the circle to complete another drawing.

Draw a straight line . . .

1. Four spaces south.
2. One space west.
3. Three spaces north.

4. One space west.
5. One space north.
6. Two spaces east.

What number did you draw? _____

Is It North, South, East, or West?

Name _____

Direction words can help you locate places quickly on a map.

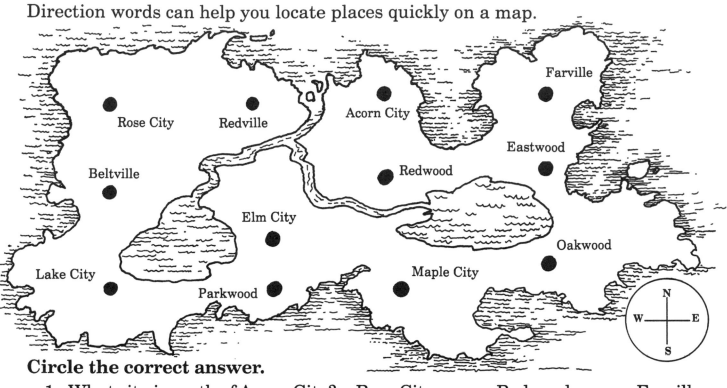

Circle the correct answer.

1. What city is south of Acorn City?	Rose City	Redwood	Farville
2. What city is north of Beltville?	Rose City	Redwood	Lake City
3. What city is east of Rose City?	Beltville	Lake City	Redville
4. What city is west of Maple City?	Redwood	Acorn City	Parkwood
5. What city is south of Farville?	Acorn City	Eastwood	Redville
6. What city is west of Redwood?	Eastwood	Maple City	Beltville
7. What city is north of Lake City?	Beltville	Maple City	Oakwood
8. What city is north of Oakwood?	Eastwood	Maple City	Lake City
9. What city is south of Elm City?	Farville	Redville	Parkwood
10. What city is west of Farville?	Acorn City	Oakwood	Eastwood

Use crayons or markers to follow these directions.

1. Draw a line south from Farville to Eastwood.
2. Draw a line north from Maple City to Redwood.
3. Draw a line east from Beltville to Redwood.
4. Draw a line west from Redville to Rose City.
5. Place an **A** on the city directly south of Eastwood.
6. Place a **B** on the city east of Acorn City.
7. Place a **C** on the first city directly north of Lake City.

Finding Your Way Around Town

Name _____

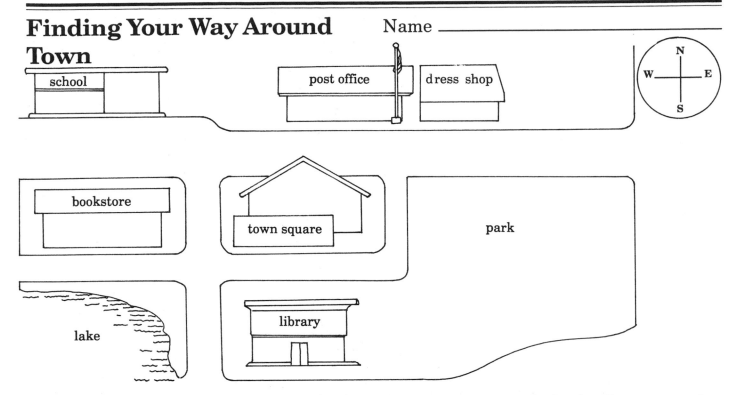

Pretend you are in the middle of the town square and circle the correct answer.

1. What direction is the library from you?   North   West   South
2. What direction is the bookstore from you?   West   East   South
3. What direction must you go to reach the post office?   East   North   West
4. Which direction must you go to get to the park?   North   West   East

Use crayons or markers to complete the map.

1. Place a red **X** on the first object north of the library.
2. Place a black **X** on the object east of the post office.
3. Draw a red circle on the object west of the dress shop.
4. Draw a blue fish on the object south of the bookstore.
5. Draw three trees east of the library.
6. Draw a movie theater east of the dress shop.
7. Draw a car south of the dress shop.
8. Draw a slide east of the school and west of the post office.
9. Draw doors and windows on the first building north of the lake.
10. Draw a yellow bus south of the object which is west of the post office.

Intermediate Directions

Concept: Intermediate directions on a map help people locate specific things or places more quickly.

Objective: To show that intermediate directions are northeast, northwest, southeast, and southwest.

Vocabulary: intermediate directions, magnetic North Pole, compass, North Pole

Background Information:
   The four basic cardinal directions on a map are north, south, east, and west.
   - Halfway between these four main directions are the four intermediate directions – northeast, northwest, southeast, and southwest. Since very few points or objects on the Earth's surface lie exactly north, south, east, or west of one another, intermediate directions are necessary.
   - When a compass points north, it is not pointing "true" north. The compass needle is attracted to the magnetic North Pole, which is not located exactly at the geographical North Pole. Only ship and airplane navigators need to worry about this small difference.
   - A compass rose on a map points to the geographical North Pole. Once north is established, all other directions fall logically into place.

Teaching Suggestions

1. Review the cardinal directions. Using a globe, point out the North Pole to the class. Explain that cartographers describe the location of places in relation to the North Pole. For instance, California is farther south than Oregon because Oregon is closer to the North Pole. When you are sure the students understand and can use cardinal directions, draw a new compass rose on the board showing intermediate directions. Explain that intermediate directions are halfway between the main directions. These directions make it easier for people to locate places or things more accurately on a map. Use the activity page *Using Intermediate Directions* at this time.

2. Prior to using the activity page *Locating Cities,* you may wish to review the cardinal and intermediate directions on a map of the United States. Ask the class to decide which direction one state is from another. For example, Arkansas is "northwest" of Mississippi; Texas is "southwest" of Arkansas.

3. The activity page *Draw Your Own Map* allows the students to become cartographers. If you stress the word *cartographer*, they will likely do a better job. Allow time for all students to complete the maps. Display these on the bulletin board with pictures of well-known cartographers/explorers to help reinforce your students' self-esteem.

Additional Activities

1. Give every two students a written set of directions from the classroom door to a pre-selected spot on the school grounds or in the school building. Stagger each pair's exit by a minute or so. This will keep the students from playing "follow the leader." You might want to post four or five helpers at various locations to assist anyone who needs help. You will have to establish the location of north for the students before they begin. You may wish to place a basket holding secret messages or small prizes for children to find when they reach their destination.

2. On a rainy day, you could play a form of "20 Questions" in your classroom. Begin the game by selecting an object in the room. The students should attempt to discover its location by asking direction questions. All questions can only be answered by yes or no. Students must always include a specific direction in their question; for instance, "Is the object north of the filing cabinet?" As the students become more knowledgeable about the directions, allow them to take your place. In the beginning, you might help the students by placing signs indicating the location of the four cardinal directions at appropriate places in the room.

Using Intermediate Directions

Name _____

Intermediate directions are halfway between the four cardinal directions. Write the names of the intermediate directions correctly on the lines.

NW is _____ . NE is _____ .

SW is _____ . SE is _____ .

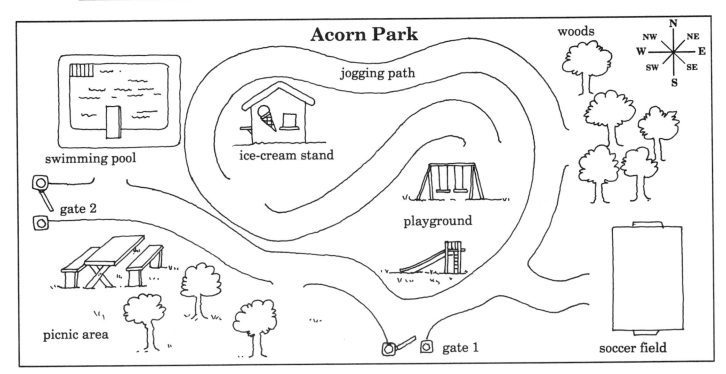

Use the names of cardinal and intermediate directions to complete these sentences about the map of Acorn Park.

1. The swimming pool is _____ of the playground.
2. The ice-cream stand is _____ of the picnic area.
3. The soccer field is _____ of the swimming pool.
4. The playground is _____ of the picnic area.
5. The woods are _____ of the playground.
6. Gate 2 is on the _____ side of Acorn Park.
7. The swimming pool is _____ of the picnic area.
8. Gate 1 is in the _____ part of Acorn Park.
9. The woods are _____ of gate 1.

Locating Cities

Name _____

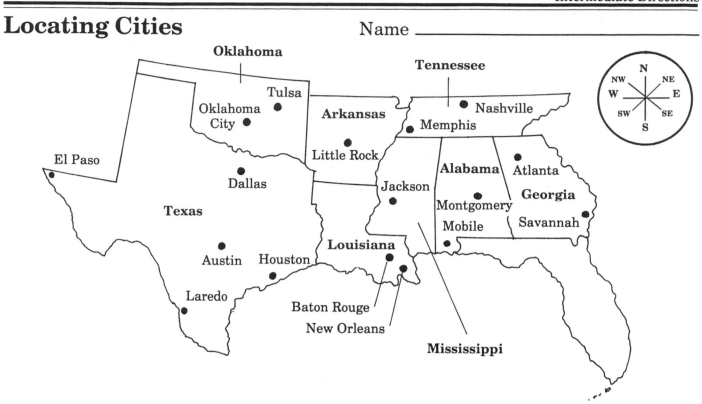

Use the compass rose to help you fill in each blank below with the correct direction.

1. El Paso, Texas, is _____ of Dallas, Texas.

2. Tulsa, Oklahoma, is _____ of Oklahoma City, Oklahoma.

3. Mobile, Alabama, is _____ of Baton Rouge, Louisiana.

4. Little Rock, Arkansas, is _____ of Nashville, Tennessee.

5. Houston, Texas, is _____ of New Orleans, Louisiana.

6. Jackson, Mississippi, is _____ of Memphis, Tennessee.

7. Dallas, Texas, is _____ of Austin, Texas.

8. The state of Louisiana is _____ of Arkansas.

9. The state of Alabama is _____ of Texas.

10. The state of Oklahoma is _____ of Tennessee.

11. The state of Georgia is _____ of Texas.

12. Atlanta, Georgia, is _____ of Savannah, Georgia.

13. The state of Tennessee is _____ of Arkansas.

14. Dallas, Texas, is _____ of Little Rock, Arkansas.

15. Mobile, Alabama, is _____ of Atlanta, Georgia.

Draw Your Own Map

Name —————————————————

A cartographer makes maps. Try your hand at being a cartographer and make your own map by following these directions. Read all directions before you begin.

1. Draw a compass rose using both cardinal and intermediate directions in the bottom right-hand corner of the map.
2. Draw a lake in the center of the map.
3. Northwest of the lake, draw some ducks in flight.
4. Directly south of the lake, draw six trees.
5. East of the ducks, draw the sun.
6. Southwest of the lake, draw a playground area.
7. East of the lake, draw a picnic area.

Picture Symbols

Concept: Cartographers sometimes use pictures to show natural and man-made features on a map.

Objective: To show that symbols on a map are pictures that stand for the real thing.

Vocabulary: symbol, explorer, picture symbol

Background Information:
- In addition to names, numbers, and directions, maps use symbols.
- Prior to the use of a written language, symbols were the only way maps could be understood. Early man drew symbols on cave walls or in the dirt to direct others to food or water.
- During the Age of Exploration, maps contained mainly symbols since the explorers could not communicate with the natives in a common tongue. They needed to show natural features, such as mountains, rivers and recognizable landmarks.
- Today cartographers still use symbols to show the location of natural and man-made features.
- Some maps use picture symbols which resemble the objects they represent. Examples:

Teaching Suggestions

1. Introduce the topic of picture symbols by asking your students if they know the symbols for a railroad crossing, a stop sign, handicapped parking, first aid, and no smoking. Have volunteers draw these symbols on the board. Explain that symbols used on a map serve the same purpose as the symbols on the board. Have the class complete the activity page *Symbols Replace Words*. The purpose of this page is to familiarize students with the various symbols which can be used on an area map.

2. Review cardinal directions. Remind the students to look for the compass rose on any map they use. On the activity page *What Do Hikers See?* the four cardinal directions are used as well as symbols.

3. The activity page *Cartographers Use Symbols* allows the student to become a cartographer. Write the word *cartographer* on the board. Ask the class to help you list the qualities needed to be a cartographer. Examples: detail-oriented (gets everything in the right spot); ability to concentrate; good memory. You may need to emphasize that with today's technology, it is not necessary for a cartographer to draw well. Computers can do this part of the job quickly and easily.

Additional Activities

1. Have students design their own symbols for objects found in the classroom or on the playground.

2. Give students a blank sheet of paper. Ask them to draw a map of the playground and design their own symbols to represent natural and man-made features. Tell them not to forget to include a compass rose.

3. Give students a sheet of paper with ten common symbols pictured. The class can be divided into groups of four or five students. Each group should redesign five of the symbols on the page. Their new designs must be easily recognizable.

Symbols Replace Words   Name _____

Symbols on a map show you where things are located.

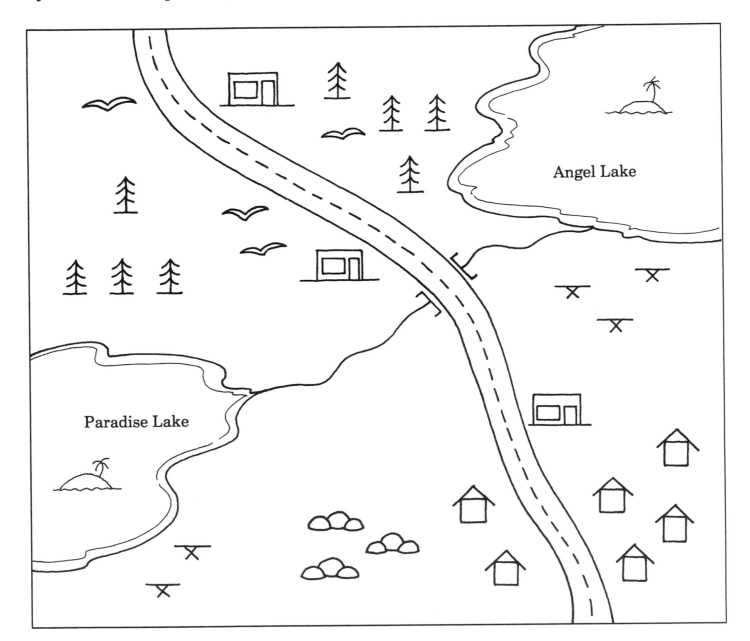

Use crayons or markers to follow these directions.

1. Color the islands brown.
2. Color the trees green.
3. Color the rocks black.
4. Color the houses blue.

5. Color the stores orange.
6. Color the birds black.
7. Color the picnic tables red.
8. Color the center lines in the road yellow.

What Do Hikers See?

Name _____

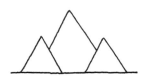

Follow the directions to complete this area map.

1. Draw a west of the 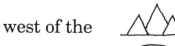 .

2. Draw 6 south of the .

3. Draw an  in the middle of the .

4. Draw 10 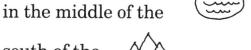 south of the 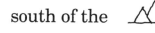 .

5. Draw a  between the 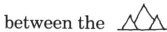 and .

6. Draw 2  on the east side of the .

7. Draw 2 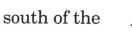 south of the 6 .

8. Draw 3 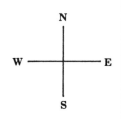 south of the .

Cartographers Use Symbols   Name _____

On another sheet of paper, draw a map using the symbols and directions given below.

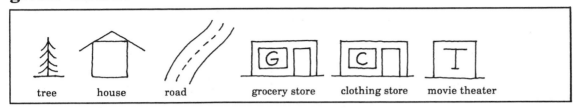

tree   house   road   grocery store   clothing store   movie theater

1. Draw a compass rose in the lower right-hand corner of the page.

2. Draw a [road symbol] in the center of your paper from west to east.

3. Draw 6 [house symbol] in the southwest corner of the map.

4. Draw 4 [tree symbol] east of the [house symbol].

5. Draw a [G grocery store] northeast of the [road symbol].

6. Draw a [C clothing store] west of the [G grocery store].

7. Draw a [T movie theater] northwest of the [road symbol].

8. Draw a [C clothing store] north of the [house symbol].

9. Draw a [G grocery store] east of the [tree symbol].

10. Draw a [G grocery store] north of the [T movie theater].

On another sheet of paper, draw another map by using the symbols and directions given below.

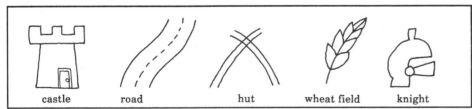

castle   road   hut   wheat field   knight

1. Draw a compass rose in the lower right-hand corner of the page.
2. Draw a castle in the center of the page.
3. Draw a road from the castle door southeast to the bottom of the page.
4. Draw 4 huts west of the castle.
5. Draw a knight on the east and west sides of the castle door.
6. Draw a wheatfield east of the castle.
7. Draw a road east from the huts to the castle road.

Map Legend

Concept: A map legend explains the specific abstract symbols used on a particular map.

Objective: To show students that a legend helps them read abstract symbols used on a map.

Vocabulary: legend, abstract, contiguous, key

Background Information:
- Abstract symbols are used to represent natural and man-made features on a map.
- Abstract symbols allow many features to be shown in a little space.
- Unlike picture symbols, abstract symbols are not always easily recognizable.
- Map legends were added as a way to explain specific abstract symbols. For example, without a legend it is impossible to know whether a ⚥ equals 100 women or 15 boys.
- Just as a compass rose is necessary to understand directions, a legend is needed to understand abstract symbols.
- A map legend is often called a *key*.

Teaching Suggestions

1. Review the concept of abstract symbols with the class. Tell the students that a legend explains specific symbols used on a map. Draw a compass rose and a legend box on the board. Help the students understand that a legend box on a map is as important as a compass rose; each helps us understand the map. Without the legend or compass rose you could not truly use the map. You may wish to use the legend box from the activity page *Legends Help You Read Maps* as an example. Then have the students complete the page.

2. Draw a circle and a square on the board. Ask the class to help you list all of the things these two shapes could stand for on a map. After they have a chance to guess, explain that the shapes can stand for anything the car-tographer chooses and are called abstract symbols. A legend box is so important that without it, it would be impossible to know what the cartographer had in mind. On the activity page *How Many People?* the students will use symbols which represent the number of people in a town or city. It may be helpful to place these symbols on the board where everyone can see them. You may wish to complete the first question on the activity page together as a class. After you are sure the students understand, have them finish the page on their own.

3. The activity page *Products in the United States* contains a map of the 48 contiguous states and uses both picture symbols and a map legend. It shows some products grown or produced in various states.

Additional Activities

1. Have students draw a map of an area in your town. Their map should include a compass rose, symbols, and a legend box.

2. This might be a good time to have students make a product map of their own state. First have the class name the products produced by your state. Write them on the board. Copy blank map outlines of your state for the class to use. Then have them place the products in the correct location on the map.

Legends Help You
Read Maps

Name _____

Use the legend box to answer the questions.

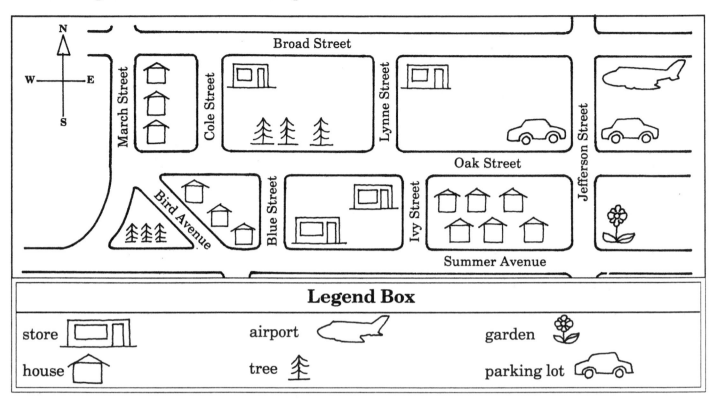

1. Does Star City have an airport? _____
2. How many houses are on Bird Avenue? _____
3. What is on the corner of Oak Street and Jefferson Street? _____
4. The garden is on the corner of Jefferson Street and _____ .
5. How many stores are in Star City? _____
6. What direction is Summer Avenue from Oak Street? _____
7. Which street is directly west of Ivy Street? _____
8. How many trees are north of Oak Street? _____
9. How many houses are between Ivy Street and Jefferson Street? _____
10. How many stores are north of Summer Avenue? _____
11. How many parking lots are east of Lynne Street? _____
12. What street is south of the garden? _____
13. What two items are found in the block between Lynne Street and Jefferson Street? _____
14. How many houses are there in all on this map? _____

How Many People?   Name _____

This map uses abstract symbols to show how many people live in each town. Use this map and the legend to answer the questions below.

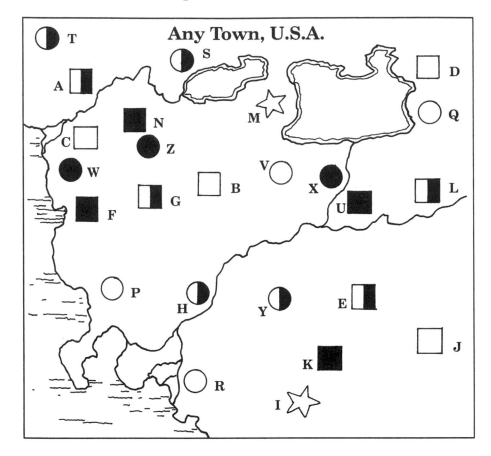

1. How many people live in a town that has this symbol ☐ ? _____
2. What does ☆ mean on the map? _____
3. Name the four towns with 0 – 500 people. _____
4. How many towns have 1,000 – 5,000 people? _____
5. How many people are in town G? _____
6. Circle the town with the most people.   A   B   I
7. Circle the town with the least people.   L   K   J
8. Name the towns with 1,000 – 5,000 people. _____
9. How many towns have over 100,000 people? _____
10. Name the towns with 50,000 – 100,000 people. _____
11. Draw a circle around the towns with 500–1,000 people. _____
12. Put a large **X** on the towns with 25,000–50,000 people. _____

Products in the United States

Name _____

Use the map and the legend box to answer the questions.

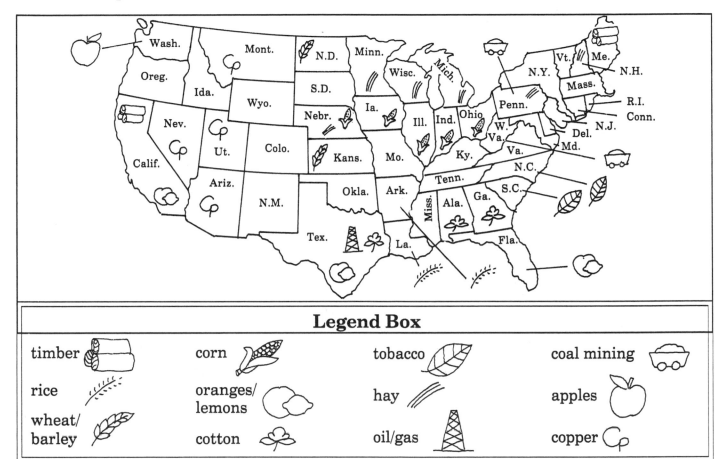

Legend Box

timber	corn	tobacco	coal mining
rice	oranges/lemons	hay	apples
wheat/barley	cotton	oil/gas	copper

1. Which state grows apples? _____
2. How many states on this map grow oranges and lemons? _____
3. Both Arkansas and Louisiana grow _____ .
4. Wheat and barley are grown in _____ .
5. North and South Carolina both grow _____ .
6. _____ is produced in Maine.
7. Name the product grown in Alabama and Georgia. _____
8. Coal is mined in the states of _____ .
9. Name the states which grow corn. _____
10. Name the products produced in California. _____
11. What crop is grown in Florida? _____
12. What crop is grown in Minnesota, Wisconsin, and Michigan? _____

Scale

Concept: A scale is a way to measure distance on a map.

Objective: To demonstrate how a scale shows distance on a map.

Vocabulary: scale, distance, junction

Background Information:
- Maps are not the same size as the places they show. Since maps cannot show real distance between places or things, a scale must be used.
- A map uses a scale to show how far apart and how large things really are. Without a scale, it would not be possible to figure how far it is from one town to another or how large a piece of land is.
- A cartographer uses a scale to reduce land and oceans proportionately on a piece of paper.
- Scales use one unit of measurement to stand for another unit of measurement.

Teaching Suggestions

1. Ask students to explain the uses of a ruler. A scale is like a ruler. It is used to measure distance. It is best if all students have a 12-inch ruler for this lesson. Before using the activity page *Measuring Distance on a Map*, let the students measure the top of their desk, an eraser, a shelf on a bookcase, or any other readily available object. This short activity will help to motivate the students for the lesson. It will also allow you to check on their understanding of a ruler.

2. The activity page *How Far Is It?* uses miles instead of feet. The students will measure the miles between cities on a map.

3. Activity page *Camping in Nature Park* also uses miles. Explain to the class the need to measure from dot to dot in a straight line. Explain the difference between actual miles and approximate miles. The nature trail is not a straight path. A ruler only allows you to measure a straight line.

4. The activity page *Traveling on Different Roads* is a road map. Students must use the compass rose, legend box, and scale to answer the questions. Explain the difference between the three types of roads found on the map:

U.S. highways are big highways linking cities across the country. They are regulated and maintained by the federal government.

State roads are roads linking towns and cities within a state. These are the responsibility of a particular state.

Local roads are smaller roads around towns or out in the county. They are usually maintained by the local town or county government.

5. Students become airline pilots while doing the activity page *Flying from Place to Place*. Airline pilots must file a flight plan with the airport before they take off. Flight plans include place and time of departure and place and time of arrival at the destination. They must also know the number of miles between places to determine the amount of fuel needed for the trip.

Additional Activities

1. Obtain copies of road maps for your state. Try to get enough for every two students. Have each pair figure the distance from their home town to other towns in the state. It will be easier if you select the towns ahead of time.

2. Assign a different state to each student. Have them write letters to the Parks and Tourism Department of their assigned state requesting a tourism map or state road map. Have each student make a chart of interesting information they glean from the maps to share with the class. Some possible information they may include on the chart: number of cities on U.S. highways; number of rivers; number of state roads; state motto; state flower; state parks; state museums, etc.

Measuring Distance on a Map

Name _____

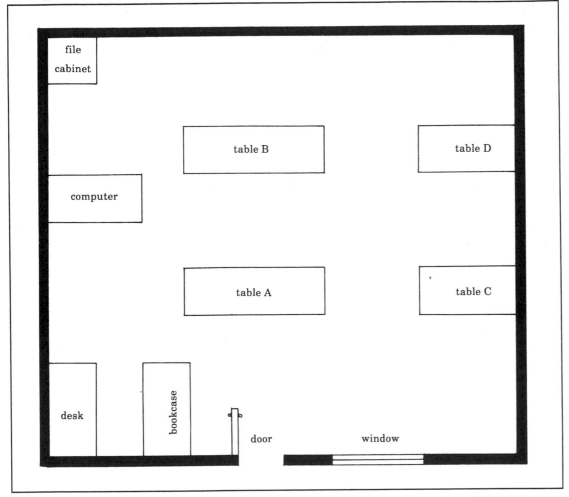

Use a ruler to help you answer these questions.

1. According to the scale, how many feet equal 1 inch? _____

2. How many feet is table A from the door? _____

3. How far is the file cabinet from the desk? _____

4. How far is table B from table D? _____

5. How many feet is the classroom from the west wall to the east wall? _____

6. How far is the door from the window? _____

7. How wide is the window? _____

8. How far is the computer from the desk? _____

9. Draw another desk 5 feet south of table C.

10. Draw another bookcase 30 feet east of the file cabinet.

How Far Is It?

Name _____

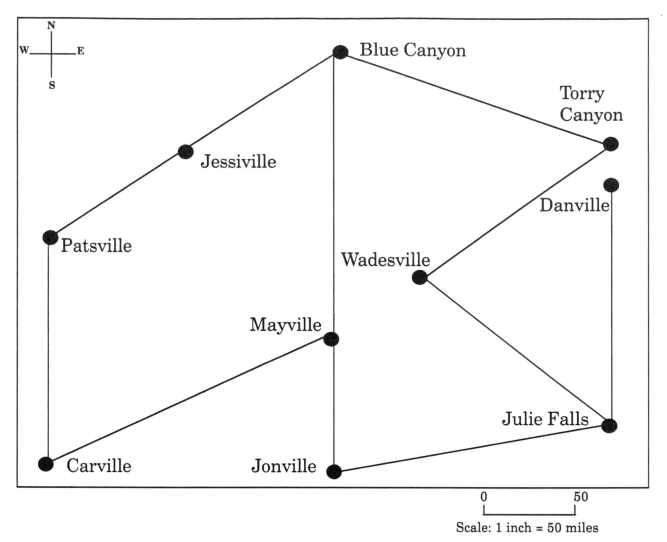

Scale: 1 inch = 50 miles

Use a ruler to measure these distances and answer the questions below.

1. How far is it from Carville to Mayville? _____

2. How far is it from Wadesville to Torry Canyon? _____

3. If you travel from Blue Canyon to Jonville, how far will you travel? _____

4. What town is between Patsville and Blue Canyon? _____

5. If you go through Wadesville, how far is it from Torry Canyon to Julie Falls?

_____

6. Which is longer – going from Carville to Patsville, or Carville to Mayville?

_____

7. Which is shorter – going from Jonville to Mayville, or Jessiville to Blue Canyon?

_____

Camping in Nature Park   Name _____

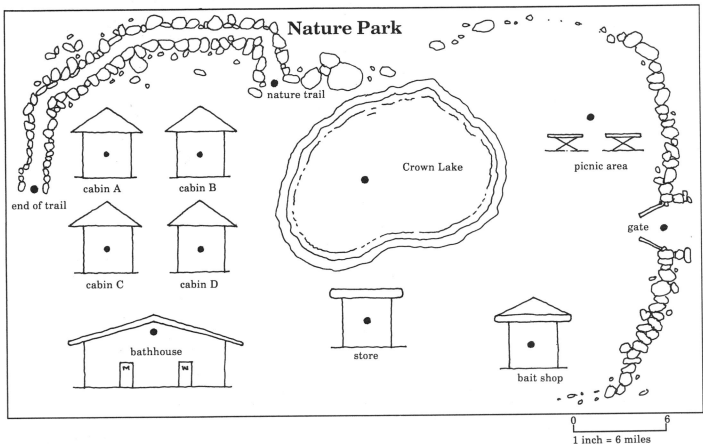

Nature Park

nature trail

Crown Lake

picnic area

cabin A   cabin B

end of trail

gate

cabin C   cabin D

bathhouse
M   W

store

bait shop

0 _____ 6
1 inch = 6 miles

Use a ruler to help you answer these questions. Measure from dot to dot.

1. How far is it from the center of Crown Lake to the bait shop? _____

2. How far is it from the picnic area to Crown Lake? _____

3. How far must you travel from cabin C to the bathhouse? _____

4. What is the distance from the nature trail to Crown Lake? _____

5. Your family is staying in cabin A. How far must you travel from the gate to the cabin? _____

6. What is the approximate distance in miles from the beginning to the end of the nature trail? _____

7. How far must your family travel to the store if you are staying in cabin D? _____

8. How far is it from the store to cabin B? _____

9. The end of the nature trail is how far from the picnic area? _____

10. How far is the bathhouse from cabin A? _____

Traveling on Different Roads   Name _____

Use a ruler to measure distance on this map and answer the questions below. Don't forget to use the compass rose and the legend box.

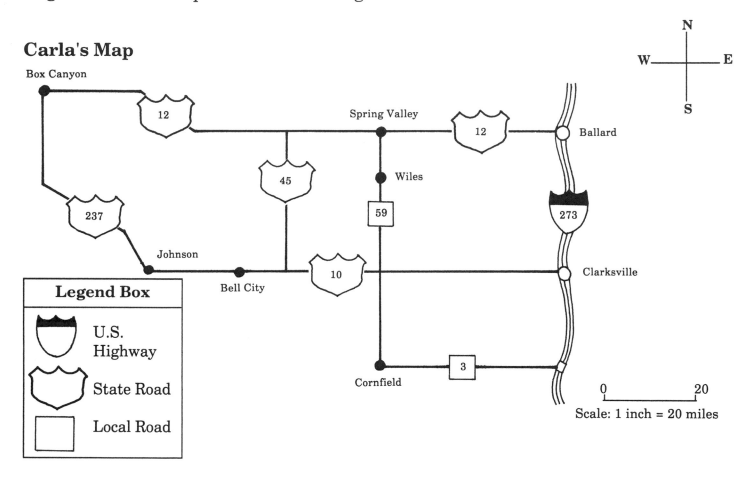

Carla's Map

1. What U.S. highway would you travel on from Clarksville to Ballard? _____
2. If Carla travels from Bell City to Clarksville, what state road will she use?

   _____
3. How far is it from Johnson to Bell City? _____
4. Do you take a state or local road to travel from Wiles to Spring Valley? _____
5. Cornfield is located at the junction of which two local roads? _____

   _____
6. How far is it from Cornfield to Clarksville? _____
7. What direction is Johnson from Bell City? _____
8. If you plan a trip from Clarksville to Ballard, what direction will you be traveling? _____
9. Trace Carla's route in red if she goes from Box Canyon to Spring Valley to Wiles.

Flying from Place to Place   Name _____

Pretend you are an airline pilot for this activity. You will need a ruler.

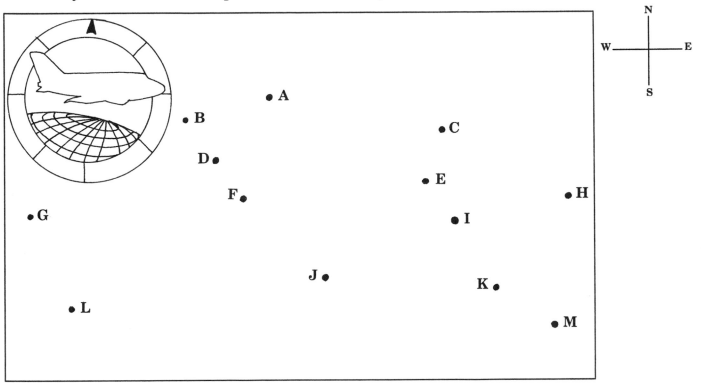

Scale
0 _____ 400
1 inch = 400 miles

1. You need to file a flight plan from city **J** to city **C.** How far will the plane travel? _____

2. You must fly from city **D** to city **F** to city **E.** How many miles will you travel? _____

3. How far is it from city **H** to city **C**? _____

4. Is it closer to fly from city **I** to city **M** or from city **I** to city **A**? _____

5. If your plane holds enough fuel to fly 500 miles, can you fly from city **L** to city **G** without refueling? _____

6. With fuel for 500 miles, can you fly from city **A** to city **J**? _____

7. About how many miles is it from city **C** to city **M**? _____

8. What direction must you fly from city **H** to city **F**? _____

9. What direction must you fly from city **J** to city **K**? _____

Grids

Concept: A map grid helps people locate places quickly on a map.

Objective: To show students how a map grid will help them locate places on a map.

Vocabulary: grid, location, coordinates, intersect, horizontal, vertical

Background Information:
- The primary function of a map is to help people locate places or objects.
- Giving correct directions means comparing the location of one place to another.
- Every place on the earth which has a permanent location can be shown on a map.
- Cartographers place two sets of lines on a map. Horizontal lines (east-west) which are lettered and vertical lines (north-south) which are numbered. These lines intersect and form a grid pattern.
- City blocks usually form a grid of their own.

Teaching Suggestions

1. As an introduction to the topic of grids, draw the intersecting lines used in a game of tic-tac-toe. Ask someone to explain the way these lines are used in the game. You may have students play one game on the board.

2. Draw this example on the board:

```
      1  2  3
    ┌──┬──┬──┐
 A  │  │  │  │
 B  ├──┼──┼──┤
 C  └──┴──┴──┘
```

Place a triangle in the "A1" space. The location of the triangle can be stated as the northwest corner or the upper left-hand corner. Explain that we are using intersecting lines or coordinates to pinpoint location. The coordinates for the triangle are "A1." Draw other shapes in various spaces. Continue doing this until you believe students understand the concept.

3. The activity page *Numbers and Letters on a Map* uses a map of city blocks. You may want to help the class with the first question.

4. The activity page *Using a Grid* is an area map. Review coordinates before doing this page.

5. The activity page *The Southern States* is a map of the southern United States. Explain again that cartographers use grid lines on a map to help with location. You may want to review boundaries with the class before using this activity sheet.

6. Activity pages *Creating Your Own Grid Map* and *Getting to Pirates' Island* provide reinforcement of grid lines and review the use of symbols and legends.

Additional Activities

1. If the students are having a difficult time understanding how grids work, have them draw the example given in **Teaching Suggestions** on their own paper. Then give these directions orally: Draw a boat in "A 3"; a balloon in "C 1"; a stick figure in "B 2"; an apple in "B 1"; a car in "A 2"; a triangle in "C 3"; a banana in "A 1"; a flower in "C 2."

2. As a variation on the first activity, use colors to fill in the spaces. Example: Color "A 1" black; color "C 2" green; color "B 1" blue, etc.

3. The students could work in pairs to create an activity similar to the pirate ship in the activity page *Getting to Pirates' Island*. Run off copies of a blank grid on construction paper. Let the students take it from there.

Numbers and Letters on a Map

Name _____

This is a map of Red Falls. Use the numbers and letters to help you answer the questions.

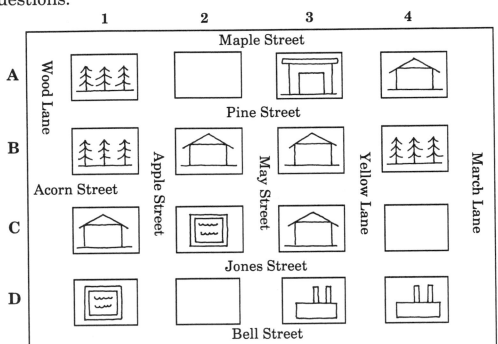

1. Locate these blocks. Write down what you see in each block.

   "A 1"_____   "C 1" _____

   "D 4"_____   "D 1" _____

   "B 2"_____   "A 3" _____

2. Name the blocks with swimming pools. _____

3. Name the blocks with houses. _____

4. Name the blocks with woods. _____

5. Tell what is located in the first block south of "A 3." _____

6. What is in the block south of "C 1"? _____

7. How many houses are in "B 2"? _____

8. How many houses altogether are in the "C" blocks? _____

9. What is in the block east of "B 3"? _____

10. What is in the block west of "D 4"? _____

11. Draw a swimming pool in "A 2."

12. Draw a house in "D 2."

13. Draw a factory in "C 4."

Using a Grid

Name _____

A map grid helps people locate places easily. Use the numbers and letters to help you answer the questions.

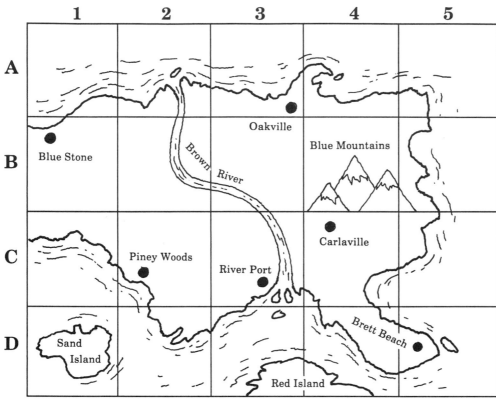

1. In which block is Brett Beach? _____

2. In which block is Blue Stone? _____

3. In which block is Piney Woods? _____

4. In which two blocks is Red Island? _____

5. In which four blocks is the Brown River? _____

6. In which block is Carlaville? _____

7. In which two blocks are the Blue Mountains? _____

8. Name the town located in "A 3." _____

9. Name the two islands found on the map. _____

10. Name the city directly north of "D 4." _____

11. In "C 5," add a town to the map. _____

12. In "B 2," add some trees. _____

13. In "A 5," add an island and name the island.

14. Draw a boat in "D 2."

15. Draw some tents in "C 1."

The Southern States

Name _____

Use the grid to help you locate places on this map of the southern United States.

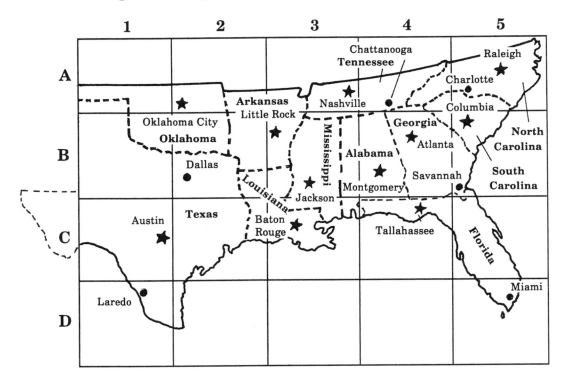

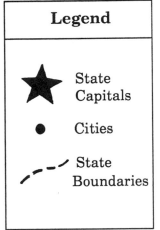

Legend

★ State Capitals

• Cities

- - - State Boundaries

1. Draw a symbol for a state capital. _____
2. What do these lines - - - - stand for? _____
3. Name the Florida city located in "D 5." _____
4. Name the state capital located in "A 3." _____
5. Give the location of Laredo, Texas. _____
6. Which state capital is located in "A 5"? _____
7. What is the location of Atlanta, Georgia? _____
8. Name the state capital located in "C 3." _____
9. Give the location of Jackson, Mississippi. _____
10. What state capital is located in "A 2"? _____
11. Give the location of Austin, Texas. _____
12. Name the city located in "B 2." _____
13. Name the cities located in "B 4._____
14. Name the state located in "A 4" and "A 5." _____
15. On this map, which three states border Texas? _____
16. Name the state east of Georgia. _____
17. Alabama and Georgia are bordered on the south by what state? _____
18. Name the Tennessee city found in "A 4". _____
19. Name the two North Carolina cities located in "A 5." _____

Creating Your Own Grid Map

Name _____

Look at the legend box. Create your own symbols for each object listed. Then follow the directions below. The first one is already done for you.

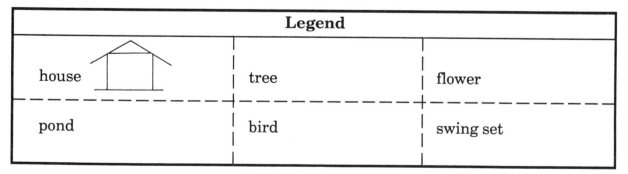

	1	2	3	4	5
A					
B					
C			🏠		
D					
E					

Legend		
house 🏠	tree	flower
pond	bird	swing set

1. Draw a house in "C3."
2. Draw a pond in "D 5" and "E 5."
3. Draw two birds in "A 2."
4. Draw one bird in "A 4."
5. Draw a tree in "C 1" and "B 1."
6. Draw a swing set in "E 3" and "E 4."
7. Draw two flowers in "D 2."
8. Draw a tree in "B 5" and "C 5."

 IF8551 Map Skills

Getting to Pirates' Island   Name _____

Pretend you are a pirate captain on your way home to Pirates' Island. Draw a picture of your ship in the box and cut it out. Place the ship on the large **X**.

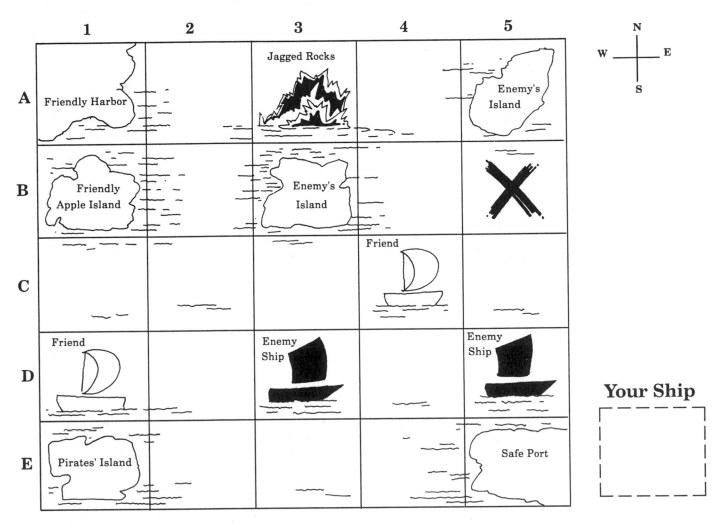

1. In which space is your ship located? _____
2. If you move your ship west two spaces, will you be safe? _____
3. Name the 5 spaces where your ship will not be safe. _____
4. What is located in space "B 1"? _____
5. Move your ship from "B 5" to "B 2." Are you in a safe space? _____
6. Move your ship south three spaces from "B 2." What is your location? _____
7. If you move your ship from "E 2" to "E1," where will you be? _____
8. Give the location for both enemy ships. _____
9. Can you safely move two spaces east of Friendly Apple Island? _____

Parallels of Latitude

Concept: Parallels of latitude are imaginary lines which help people locate places north and south of the equator.

Objective: To demonstrate that latitude is a series of imaginary lines used by people to locate places north and south of the equator.

Vocabulary: parallel, latitude, hemisphere, equator

Background Information:
- Cartographers use imaginary lines on a map to help people locate places. These lines form a grid by the means of which any place on earth can be located. Latitude lines measure a place's location north or south of the equator.
- The best known latitude line is the equator. The equator marks the middle of the earth. All other latitude lines are parallel to the equator. They run the same direction and are always the same distance apart.
- Latitude lines are also called *parallels of latitude.*
- The distance between latitude lines which are 1° apart is about 70 miles.
- Parallels of latitude are continuous rings around the earth. They run east to west, but are measured north and south of the equator. The word *latitude* is derived from Latin meaning *breadth* or *width.*

Teaching Suggestions

1. Review the grid system from the previous lesson. Explain that cartographers use imaginary lines to help locate places on a map. Point to the equator on a world map. The equator is a continuous imaginary ring around the earth. The equator divides the earth into two parts, or Hemispheres, called Northern and Southern. Other latitude lines are parallel to the equator and are also called parallels of latitude. Half are north of the equator and half are south. Parallels of latitude are measured in units called degrees (°). The equator is always 0° latitude. All other parallels of latitude **must** show whether they are north or south. The activity page *Imaginary Lines* will acquaint the students with some of the major latitude lines. Prior to using this sheet, stress the importance of the words *north* and *south.* All parallels north and south of the equator use the same numbers with an **N** or **S** after to indicate the direction from the equator.

2. The next three activity pages do not show the equator. Each of these shows an area north of the equator. You should insist students **always** include a direction as part of their answer. It is very difficult to locate a place near the 50° parallel without knowing whether it is north or south.

Additional Activities

1. Have groups of four or five students create a game using parallels of latitude. The game should help others understand locating places using latitude lines.

2. Using an encyclopedia, have students design charts describing cities and the kinds of vegetation found there. Choose cities between different parallels of latitude. This should introduce students to the different types of climate found on the earth.

Imaginary Lines

Name _____

Parallels of latitude are imaginary lines north and south of the equator. They are measured in units called degrees (°). Answer the questions using these maps.

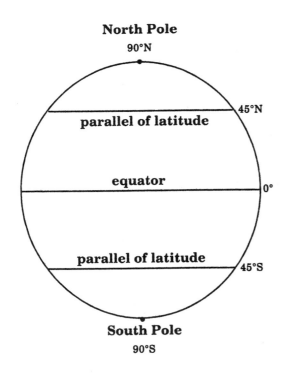

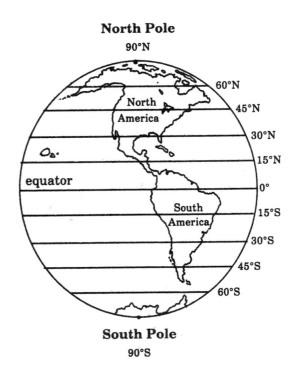

1. The _____ is 0° latitude.
2. The North Pole is _____ degrees north latitude.
3. Lines of latitude are measured in units called _____ .
4. Lines north and south of the equator are called _____ .
5. The _____ is 90°S latitude.
6. Which line is closer to the equator – 30°N or 15°S? _____
7. Which is closer to the South Pole – 45°S or 30°S? _____
8. Which is farther from the North Pole – 45°N or 15°N? _____
9. At what degree is the South Pole? _____
10. Which is farther from the equator – 30°N or 30°S? _____
11. How many degrees are between the equator and each of the poles? _____
12. If you wanted to find a city located at 45°N, would you look above or below the equator? _____
13. Which continent on the map is entirely north of the equator? _____
14. South America lies between the parallels of latitude ____N and 60°S.
15. The equator runs through the northern part of the continent of _____ .
16. Color all the land north of the equator red.
17. Color all of the land south of the equator green.

Latitude in North America

Name _____

Use with page 51.

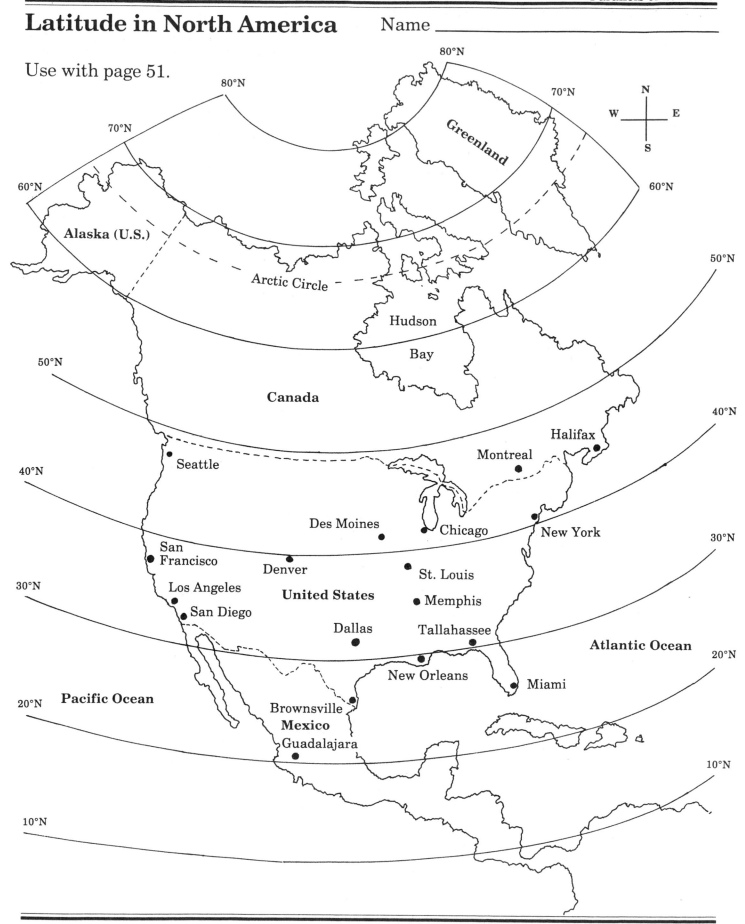

Latitude in North America   Name _____
(Continued)

Use the map on page 50 to answer these questions.

1. The Arctic Circle is located between the 60°N and _____°N.

2. Is Chicago closer to 40°N or 50°N?   _____

3. Name the three United States cities located between 20°N and 30°N.

   _____   _____

   _____

4. New York is closest to the _____ parallel of latitude.

5. Name the eight United States cities located between 30°N and 40°N.

   _____   _____

   _____   _____

   _____   _____

   _____   _____

6. The _____ Ocean is on the eastern side of the United States.

7. _____ is the country south of the United States.

8. Canada is the country _____ of the United States.

9. On the west, the United States is bordered by the _____ Ocean.

10. Montreal is in the country of _____ .

11. Seattle is located closest to the _____ parallel of latitude.

12. What part of the United States does the Arctic Circle cross?_____

13. Memphis is located between the ____ parallel and the ____ parallel.

14. Is Dallas north or south of the 30°N parallel of latitude? _____

15. Name the four United States cities located between 40°N and 50°N.

   _____   _____

   _____   _____

16. Denver is closest to the _____ parallel of latitude.

17. San Francisco is located near _____ °N.

18. Does the Arctic Circle pass through Greenland?_____

19. Which parallel of latitude on the map goes through Florida?_____

20. Guadalajara is located in what country? _____

Parallels Help with Location

Name _____

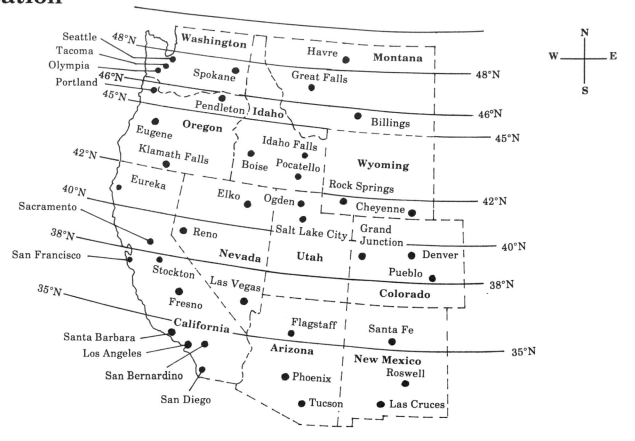

1. Billings, Montana, is which direction from the 46°N parallel? _____

2. Pueblo, Colorado, is almost directly on the _____ parallel of latitude.

3. The boundary between Oregon and California is formed by the _____ parallel.

4. The state of Wyoming is located between 41°N parallel and _____ parallel.

5. Name three cities in Idaho south of the 45°N parallel of latitude.

   _____

6. Which of these cities is south of the 35°N parallel – Flagstaff, Arizona or Roswell, New Mexico? _____

7. Name the three California cities located between the 35°N and 38°N parallels.

   _____

8. All of the cities shown in Washington are between the parallels of
   _____ and _____ .

9. Which two Nevada cities are north of the 38°N parallel? _____
   and _____

10. Klamath Falls, Oregon, is almost directly on the _____ parallel.

11. Name the four states located entirely north of the 42°N parallel.

   _____

Locating Places in Western Europe

Name _____

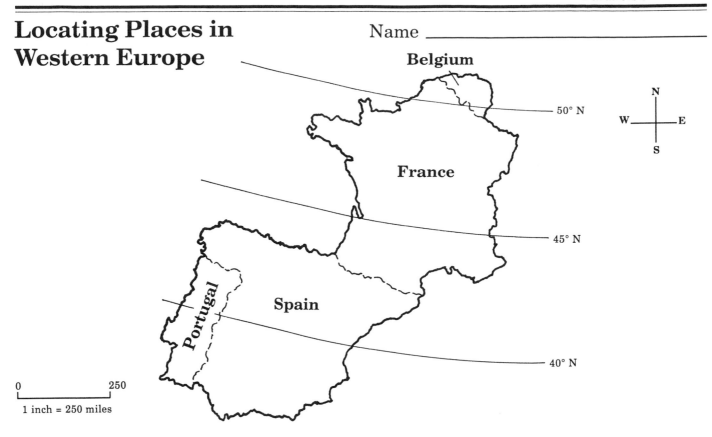

1 inch = 250 miles

1. Name the four countries on this map. _____
   _____

2. One inch equals _____ miles on the map.

3. Which parallel line crosses both Portugal and Spain? _____

4. Which two parallel lines cross France? _____

5. Name the country directly north of France. _____

6. Place the city of Barcelona on the northeastern coast of Spain about 225 miles south of the 45°N parallel.

7. Place the city of Paris in the north central part of France about 75 miles south of the 50°N parallel.

8. Place Lisbon on the western coast of Portugal about 75 miles south of the 40°N parallel.

9. Place Madrid in the center of Spain about 50 miles north of the 40°N parallel.

10. Place Brussels near the northcentral part of Belgium about 50 miles north of the 50°N parallel line.

11. Place Porto on the western coast of Portugal 75 miles north of 40°N parallel.

12. Place Toulouse in the southwestern part of France 100 miles south of the 45°N parallel.

Meridians of Longitude

Concept: Meridians of longitude are imaginary lines which help people locate places east and west of the prime meridian.

Objective: To show that meridians of longitude help people locate places east and west of the prime meridian.

Vocabulary: meridian, longitude, prime meridian, hemisphere

Background Information:
- In addition to parallels of latitude, cartographers use meridians of longitude.
- Meridians of longitude are imaginary lines that run north and south on the earth's surface dividing the earth into 360 equal parts.
- These lines are called meridians and are half circles which meet at the North and South Poles.
- The best known longitude line is the prime meridian. All places can be located east or west of the prime meridian.
- Longitude meridians are measured in degrees (°). The prime meridian is 0° longitude and passes through Greenwich, England.
- Map makers can measure up to 180° west and 180° east from the prime meridian.
- The width of each degree of longitude at the equator represents about 70 miles and becomes less and less the farther north and south you travel. At the poles there is no distance between meridians because this is where meridians meet.
- The usual boundaries between the Eastern and Western Hemispheres are drawn along the meridians of 20° W longitude and 160° E longitude.

Teaching Suggestions

1. Use a globe and a large wall map of the earth to point out the North and South Poles. Unlike parallels, meridians do meet. They meet at the North and South Poles. Each meridian is a half circle. Meridians begin and end at the Poles. The activity page *Where Is the Prime Meridian?* is an introduction to meridians. You may want to review the four cardinal directions before passing it out.

2. Some students will have trouble with the concept of longitude. Tell students over and over that meridians are measured east and west from the prime meridian. **Always** require the answers to be written correctly, including number, degree symbol, and direction letter (Example: 15° E.) Without all of the parts, the answer will not show an accurate location.

3. Use a large map of the world to show the location of the United States. As part of the Western Hemisphere, North America has a west longitude. Use the activity page *Locating Cities* at this time.

4. The activity page *North and South Dakota* provides good practice for those students who are still having problems understanding longitude.

5. The last activity page for this lesson, *Locating Cities in Europe,* is a bit more complicated. The map shows some of the countries in Europe. Remind the class of the location of the prime meridian by showing them on a large map. The prime meridian runs through Great Britain, France, and Spain. A large map of Europe will allow you to show the students why some cities in the same country are east longitude and some are west longitude.

Additional Activity

Divide the classroom in half. Have students face the chalkboard. Use a piece of string or a chalk line to divide the room into east and west longitude. Pretend the line is the prime meridian. To the right of the line is east longitude. To the left is west longitude. Choose objects on either side of the line. Have the students tell you what the object's location is – east or west longitude.

Where Is the Prime Meridian? Name _____

Meridians of longitude help people locate places east and west of the prime meridian and are measured in units called degrees (°). Complete this page and page 56.

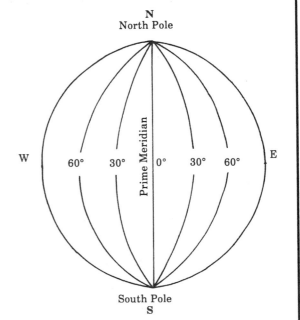

1. What do the letters **N, S, E,** and **W** stand for? _____
2. The _____ is 0° longitude.
3. Meridians of longitude are measured _____ and _____ of the prime meridian.
4. Where do all the meridians meet?

   _____
5. Meridians of longitude are measured in units called _____

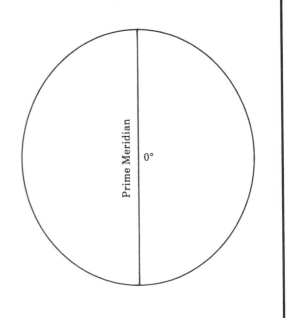

Do the following to complete this map.
(Hint: the map above will help you.)
   A. Label the four cardinal directions.
   B. Draw a meridian at 30°E and 30°W.
   C. Draw a meridian at 60°E and 60°W.
   D. Label the North and South Poles.

Where Is the Prime Meridian? (Continued)

Name _____

Use with page 55.

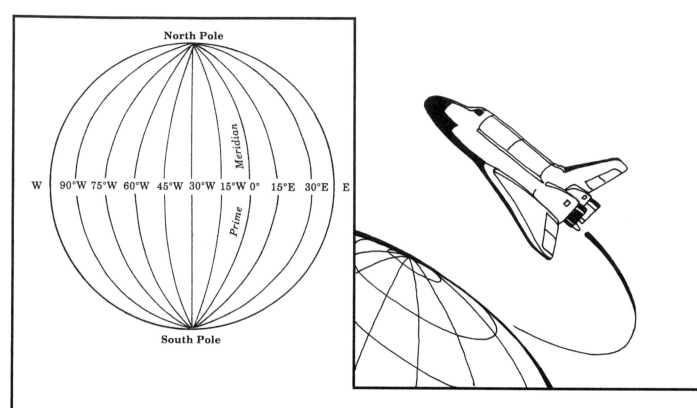

1. Is 15°E or 30°W farther from the prime meridian? _____
2. Is 60°W or 15°E closer to the prime meridian? _____
3. Name the two meridians east of the prime meridian on this map.

   _____

4. How many meridians are west of the prime meridian on this map? _____
5. On this map, what meridian is located between 15°W and 15°E?

   _____

6. Is 30°W or 15°E closer to the prime meridian? _____
7. Is 75°W or 90°W closer to the prime meridian? _____
8. Is 90°W or 15°E closer to 15°W? _____
9. Is 90°W or 75°W closer to the prime meridian? _____
10. Is 45°W or 30°E closer to the prime meridian? _____
11. Name the meridian west of 75°W. _____
12. Name the meridian east of 15°E. _____

Locating Cities

Name _____

This map shows part of the northeastern United States. All longitude meridians on this map are west.

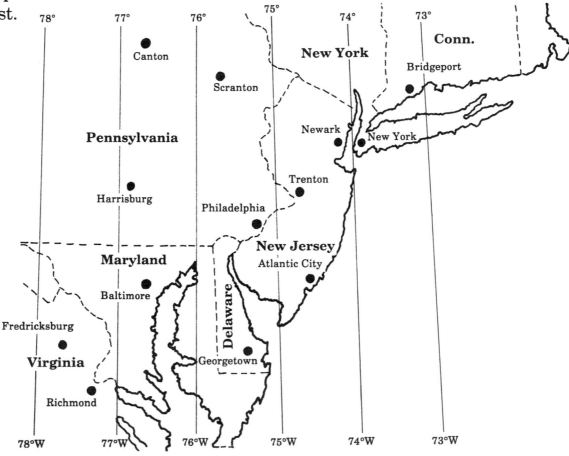

1. Bridgeport, Connecticut, is closest to which meridian? _____
2. Name the three cities located between 75°W and 76°W on this map.

   _____   _____   _____

3. Trenton, New Jersey, is closest to which meridian? _____
4. Name the meridians closest to these cities:
   Philadelphia _____   Georgetown _____
   Scranton _____   Newark _____
5. Name the seven states shown on this map.

   _____   _____   _____

   _____   _____   _____

   _____

6. Atlantic City is between _____ and _____ longitude.
7. Harrisburg is closest to which meridian? _____
8. Which is farther west: Harrisburg or Philadelphia? _____
9. Richmond is closest to _____ longitude.
10. Which is farther north: Canton or Newark? _____

North and South Dakota   Name _____

Use this map to answer the questions. All longitude meridians will be west.

1. Which meridian is closest to Eureka, South Dakota?_____
2. The people of McIntosh live in which state?_____
3. Which town is closer to 98°W – Platte, South Dakota, or Lisbon, North Dakota?

   _____

4. Grenora, North Dakota, is located almost exactly on the _____ meridian.
5. Is Deadwood, South Dakota, north or south of Rapid City? _____
6. Which town is closer to 104°W – Bowman, North Dakota, or Lemmon, South Dakota? _____
7. If you were traveling east from Rapid City, which meridian would you arrive at first? _____
8. Which meridian would you reach first when traveling east from Sioux Falls, South Dakota? _____
9. Bismarck is in the state of _____ .
10. Lemmon, South Dakota, is closest to the _____ meridian.
11. Name the North Dakota cities located east of 98°W longitude.

    _____

    _____

12. Pierre is in the state of _____ .

Locating Cities in Europe

Name _____

Use this map to answer the questions. Pay particular attention to the location of the prime meridian.

1. On the map label each longitude meridian either east or west.
2. Rome, Italy, is located between the _____ and _____ meridians.
3. Which meridian passes through the western edge of Ireland? _____
4. Portugal is located between the _____ and _____ meridians.
5. What name is given to the meridian which is 0°? _____
6. Between which two meridians is Switzerland located? _____
7. Explain how you would decide which of the 5° meridians is east and which is west.

   _____

8. Warsaw is closest to the _____ meridian.
9. Marseille, France, is which direction from the 5°E meridian? _____
10. Gdansk is in the country of _____ .
11. Dublin is on the _____ coast of Ireland.
12. Which is closer to the 15°E meridian – Naples or Venice? _____
13. Prague is _____ of 15°E longitude.
14. Hamburg is closest to the _____ meridian.
15. Marseille is almost on the _____ meridian of longitude.

Latitude and Longitude Lines

Concept: Parallels of latitude and meridians of longitude are imaginary lines used by cartographers to pinpoint the location of places and things on the earth's surface.

Objective: To demonstrate how parallels of latitude and meridians of longitude are aids used to help people locate places and things on the earth's surface.

Vocabulary: latitude, longitude, meridian, parallel, degree, coordinates

Background Information:
- Parallels of latitude and meridians of longitude are imaginary lines. They are included on maps to aid the map user in locating places or things.
- The equator is 0° latitude. All other latitude lines are north and south of the equator. Latitude lines run parallel to the equator.
- Each degree (°) of latitude equals about 70 miles.
- In addition to parallels of latitude, meridians of longitude are necessary to help people precisely locate a place on the earth's surface. Meridians of longitude are lines east or west of the prime meridian, which passes through Greenwich, England.
- The prime meridian is 0° longitude. This particular meridian was designated *the prime meridian* by a group of geographers in the 1800's.
- Halfway around the earth is the 180° meridian. On most maps this line reads E 180°W.
- At the equator the distance between each degree of longitude is approximately 70 miles. Since the meridians come closer together as they near the poles, the distance between them lessens. Halfway to the poles 1° of longitude is about 49 miles, whereas one mile from the poles, it is only 30 yards.

Teaching Suggestions

1. In the previous two lessons, the students looked at parallels of latitude and meridians of longitude separately. It is not possible to accurately locate a site on earth using only one set of lines. Both Washington, D.C., and Beijing, China, are located at 40° N latitude. They are, of course, several thousand miles apart. You must know the degree of longitude to correctly locate each city. Review latitude and longitude with the class. Use a large map of the world to again point out the equator and the prime meridian. Never fail to stress that these lines are imaginary. You will not be able to see them from an airplane or space ship. Also, be sure the students are not confusing the direction these lines run with the way they are measured. This is a common mistake made by many people. Parallels of latitude run east to west, but are **measured** north and south of the equator. Meridians of longitude run north to south, but are **measured** east and west of the prime meridian. Latitude lines begin at 0° and end at 90°. Longitude lines begin at 0° and end at 180°.

2. The activity page *Latitude and Longitude Lines* introduces the students to a map using both sets of lines. *Using Lines to Draw a State* and *Casey's Island* use grid systems to help students get accustomed to using two sets of lines. The word **coordinate** is introduced in the activity page *Four States*. Be sure you give the class the definition of **coordinate** prior to using this activity page. The rest of the activity pages may be used as you feel necessary.

Additional Activity

Make up a game using both latitude and longitude lines. On a grid similar to the one on page 62, have the students draw things at specific coordinates. For example: "Draw a star at coordinate 38°N/99°W."

Latitude and Longitude Lines

Name _____

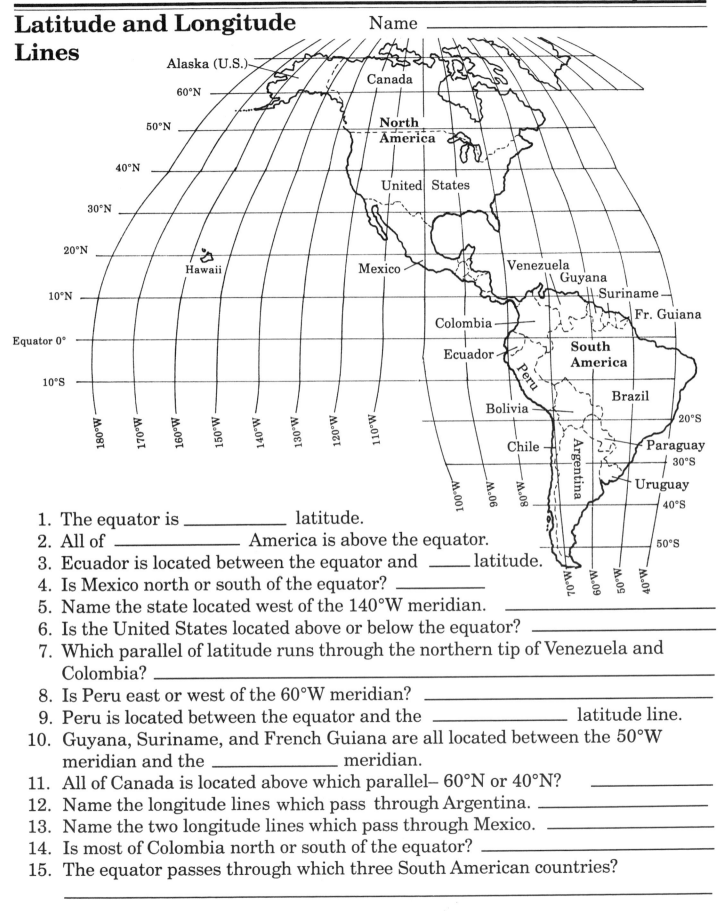

1. The equator is _____ latitude.
2. All of _____ America is above the equator.
3. Ecuador is located between the equator and ____ latitude.
4. Is Mexico north or south of the equator? _____
5. Name the state located west of the 140°W meridian. _____
6. Is the United States located above or below the equator? _____
7. Which parallel of latitude runs through the northern tip of Venezuela and Colombia? _____
8. Is Peru east or west of the 60°W meridian? _____
9. Peru is located between the equator and the _____ latitude line.
10. Guyana, Suriname, and French Guiana are all located between the 50°W meridian and the _____ meridian.
11. All of Canada is located above which parallel– 60°N or 40°N? _____
12. Name the longitude lines which pass through Argentina. _____
13. Name the two longitude lines which pass through Mexico. _____
14. Is most of Colombia north or south of the equator? _____
15. The equator passes through which three South American countries?

_____

Using Lines to Draw a State Name _____

Below is a grid system using latitude and longitude lines. Place a dot on each point given. The first two have been done for you.

1. 38°N/99°W
2. 38°N/102°W
3. 36°N/102°W
4. 34°N/102°W
5. 34°N/104°W
6. 34°N/106°W
7. 33°N/105 1/2°W
8. 32 1/2°N/105°W
9. 32°N/104 1/2°W

10. 31°N/104°W
11. 30°N/104°W
12. 29 1/2° N/103°W
13. 30°N/102°W
14. 30°N/101°W
15. 29°N/101°W
16. 28°N/100°W
17. 27 1/2°N/99°W
18. 26 1/2°N/97 1/2°W

19. 28°N/97 1/2°W
20. 29°N/96 1/2°W
21. 30°N/95°W
22. 31°N/94°W
23. 33°N/94°W
24. 35°N/94°W
25. 35°N/96°W
26. 35°N/99°W
27. 37°N/99°W

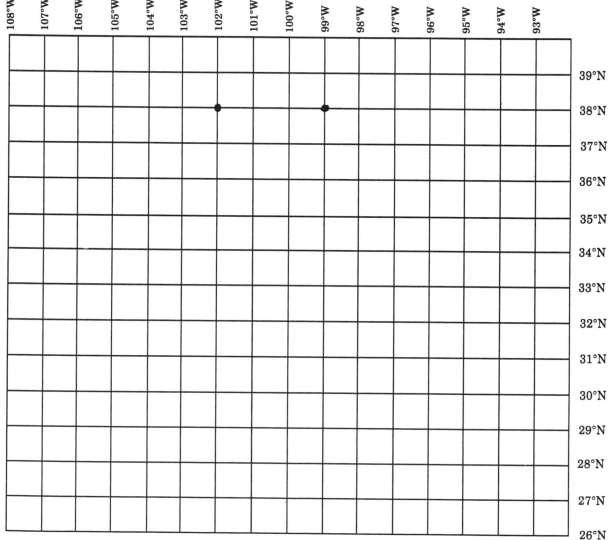

Draw a line to connect all of the dots in order. What state did you draw? _____

Casey's Island

Name _____

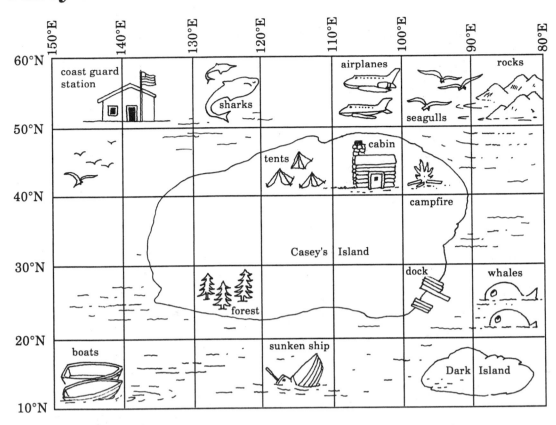

1. The whales are between which two latitude lines? _____

2. The coast guard station is located between which longitude lines?

    _____

3. If the whales go north to 55°N latitude, what will they hit? _____

4. The boats must cross what longitude lines to get to the sunken ship?

    _____

5. If the airplanes travel south across 40°N latitude, over which building will they

    pass? _____

6. If you draw a latitude line at 35°N, what will you cross? _____

7. If the whales cross 90°E longitude, what will they reach? _____

8. Name the items crossed by the 55°N latitude line. _____

    _____

9. Which island is crossed by 90°E longitude? _____

10. Which longitude lines cross Casey's Island? _____

Four States

Use this map to fill in the charts on page 65. Two answers have been filled in for you.

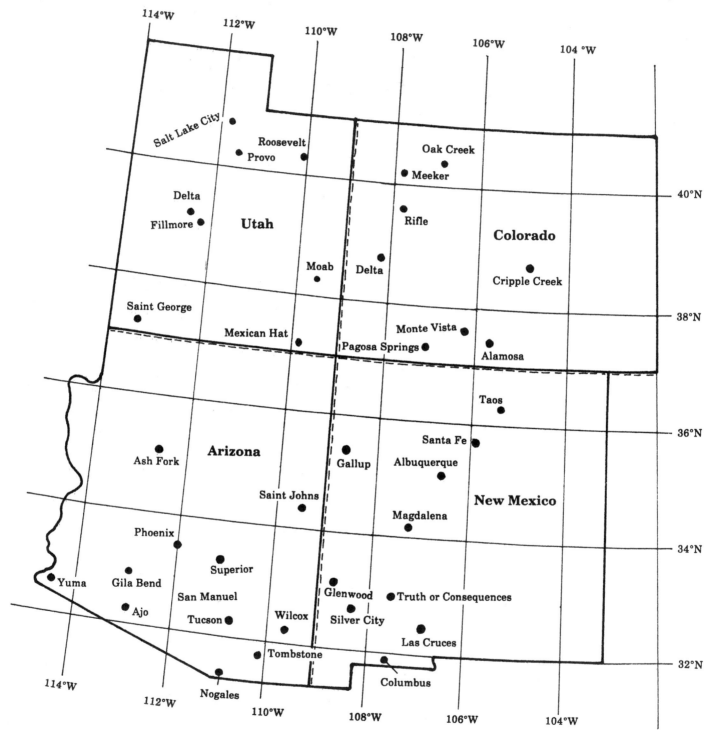

Four States (Continued)

Name _____

Use with page 64.

City	Coordinates
1. Salt Lake City, Utah	*41°N / 112°W*
2. Tucson, Arizona	
3. Santa Fe, New Mexico	
4. Oak Creek, Colorado	
5. Wilcox, Arizona	
6. Cripple Creek, Colorado	
7. Las Cruces, New Mexico	
8. Albuquerque, New Mexico	
9. Meeker, Colorado	
10. Saint George, Utah	

Coordinates	City
1. 33°N/109°W	*Glenwood*
2. 41°N/112°W	
3. 39°N/108°W	
4. 31°N/111°W	
5. 37°N/110°W	
6. 40 1/2°N/110°W	
7. 33 1/2°N/107°W	
8. 39°N/112 1/2°W	
9. 35 1/2°N/108 1/2°W	
10. 33°N/111°W	

Approximate Coordinates	State
1. 32°N/36°N and 110°W/114°W	
2. 36°N/41°N and 110°W/114°W	
3. 32°N/36°N and 104°W/108°W	
4. Color the remaining state yellow.	

Name the City

Name ——————————

Use the coordinates given below to locate each of the cities. The first one has been done for you.

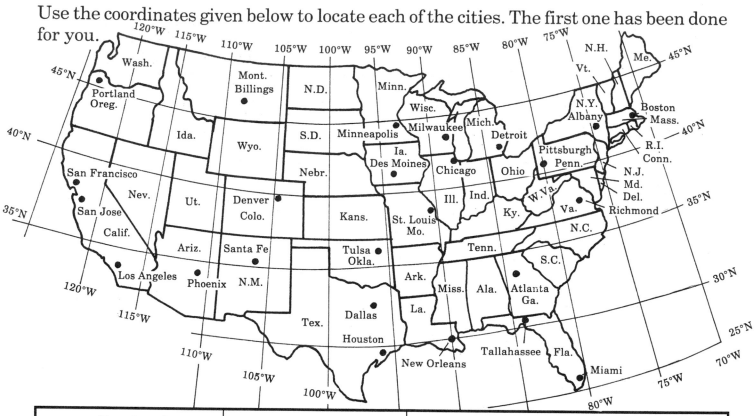

Latitude	Longitude	City
1. 34°N	84°W	*Atlanta*
2. 26°N	80°W	
3. 40°N	80°W	
4. 36°N	96°W	
5. 37°N	122°W	
6. 33°N	112°W	
7. 39°N	90°W	
8. 46°N	108°W	
9. 43°N	88°W	
10. 42°N	94°W	
11. 43°N	74°W	
12. 45°N	93°W	
13. 33°N	97°W	
14. 30°N	95°W	

Where in Europe?

Use with page 68.

Name _____

Where in Europe? (Continued)   Name _____

Estimate and write the coordinates and countries for these European cities using the map on page 67. The first one has been done for you.

City	Latitude	Longitude	Country
1. London	52°N	0°	United Kingdom
2. Belgrade			
3. Warsaw			
4. Stockholm			
5. Athens			
6. Helsinki			
7. Paris			
8. Munich			
9. Copenhagen			
10. Oslo			
11. Glasgow			
12. Prague			
13. Bern			
14. Hamburg			
15. Dresden			
16. Dublin			
17. Rome			
18. Budapest			
19. Vienna			
20. Amsterdam			

What Will They Be?

Name _____

Place a dot at each of these latitude and longitude points on the graph.

1. 45°N/105°W
2. 40°N/110°W
3. 35°N/115°W
4. 30°N/120°W
5. 25°N/125°W
6. 20°N/120°W
7. 15°N/115°W
8. 10°N/110°W

9. 5°N/105°W
10. 10°N/100°W
11. 15°N/95°W
12. 20°N/90°W
13. 25°N/85°W
14. 30°N/90°W
15. 35°N/95°W
16. 40°N/100°W

Draw a line to connect the dots in order. What have you drawn? _____

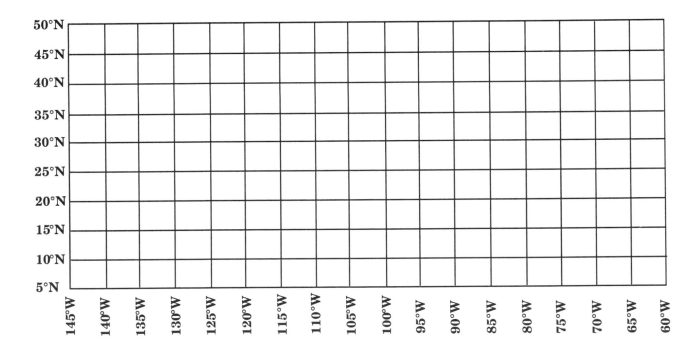

Now with a different color, place a dot at each of these latitude and longitude points.

1. 45°N/85°W
2. 35°N/85°W

3. 35°N/65°W
4. 45°N/65°W

Connect the dots. What have you drawn? _____

Physical Maps

Concept: Physical maps show the natural features and roughness of the earth.

Objective: To demonstrate that physical maps show those parts of the earth which were created by nature, not those created by humans.

Vocabulary: physical, vegetation, terrain, topography, relief, elevation, highlands, mountain, pampas, plateau, plain, lowland, coast, interior, Arctic, tundra, key

Background Information:
- Physical maps show the features of the earth created by nature. They show the vegetation and terrain, such as jungles, deserts, grasslands, and waterways.
- Sometimes physical maps are called topographical maps.
- Many cartographers use shaded relief to show the different shapes.
- Elevation of the land is also shown on physical maps. Color can be used to show the different elevations on the earth's surface. Some maps use a variety of lines to show elevation.
- The map legend, or key, tells how to read the physical map.

Teaching Suggestions

1. If possible, use a large physical map of the world to introduce the topic of physical maps. You may have problems locating one since many maps today combine physical and political features. Some encyclopedias utilize separate physical and political maps for each continent and country. You could make copies for each of the students or make a transparency to use on the overhead projector. Point out the map key to the students. (A *key* is also sometimes called a *legend*.) Without the key, you cannot accurately read the map. The activity pages in this book use various shading and lines instead of color. Students will need to refer to the key. They will also need to use the compass rose on all activity pages.

2. You may wish to introduce the topic of physical maps to the class in a vocabulary lesson. Have the students define all of the words listed in the **Vocabulary** section. Give each student his or her own copy of the glossary at the back of this book, since elementary dictionaries may not have definitions for some of the words.

3. All five activity pages present basically the same information in several different ways. They may be completed in any order.

Additional Activities

1. The activity page *Physical Features of the United States* can be colored. Have the students make a key using a different color for each natural feature.

2. The vocabulary words in the lesson could be used as spelling words.

3. Create a crossword puzzle or wordsearch with the vocabulary words for the students to enjoy.

4. Assign a different state or country to each student. Have them make a physical map showing the terrain for their state or country. This could be displayed on the outside wall of your classroom, the cafeteria, or the library. Students from other classes would benefit from the display.

Land in South America

Name ⎯⎯⎯⎯⎯⎯⎯⎯⎯⎯⎯⎯

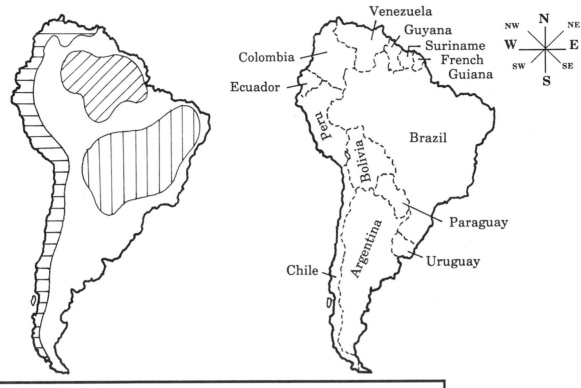

Map Key			
Brazilian Highlands	Guiana Highlands	Andes Mountains	Pampas

1. Over half of the continent is covered by ⎯⎯⎯⎯⎯⎯⎯⎯⎯⎯⎯⎯⎯ .

2. The ⎯⎯⎯⎯⎯⎯⎯⎯⎯ Mountains run from north to south on the western half of the continent.

3. In what part of the country are the Guiana Highlands located? ⎯⎯⎯⎯⎯⎯⎯

4. In the eastern part of South America is an area called the ⎯⎯⎯⎯⎯⎯⎯⎯ Highlands.

5. Most of Argentina is covered by ⎯⎯⎯⎯⎯⎯⎯⎯ .

6. The eastern part of Brazil is the ⎯⎯⎯⎯⎯⎯⎯⎯ Highlands.

7. Which country is covered completely by pampas – Uruguay or Venezuela? ⎯⎯⎯⎯

⎯⎯⎯⎯⎯⎯⎯⎯⎯⎯⎯⎯⎯⎯⎯⎯⎯⎯⎯⎯⎯⎯⎯⎯⎯⎯⎯⎯⎯⎯

8. Colombia's northeast border is formed by the country of ⎯⎯⎯⎯⎯⎯⎯⎯⎯ .

9. Name the five countries which border Argentina. ⎯⎯⎯⎯⎯⎯⎯⎯⎯⎯

⎯⎯⎯⎯⎯⎯⎯⎯⎯⎯⎯⎯⎯⎯⎯⎯⎯⎯⎯⎯⎯⎯⎯⎯⎯⎯⎯⎯⎯⎯

10. Which country does not contain the Andes Mountains within its borders – Chile, Peru, or Uruguay? ⎯⎯⎯⎯⎯⎯⎯⎯⎯

Comparing Two States

Name _____

Missouri   **Tennessee**

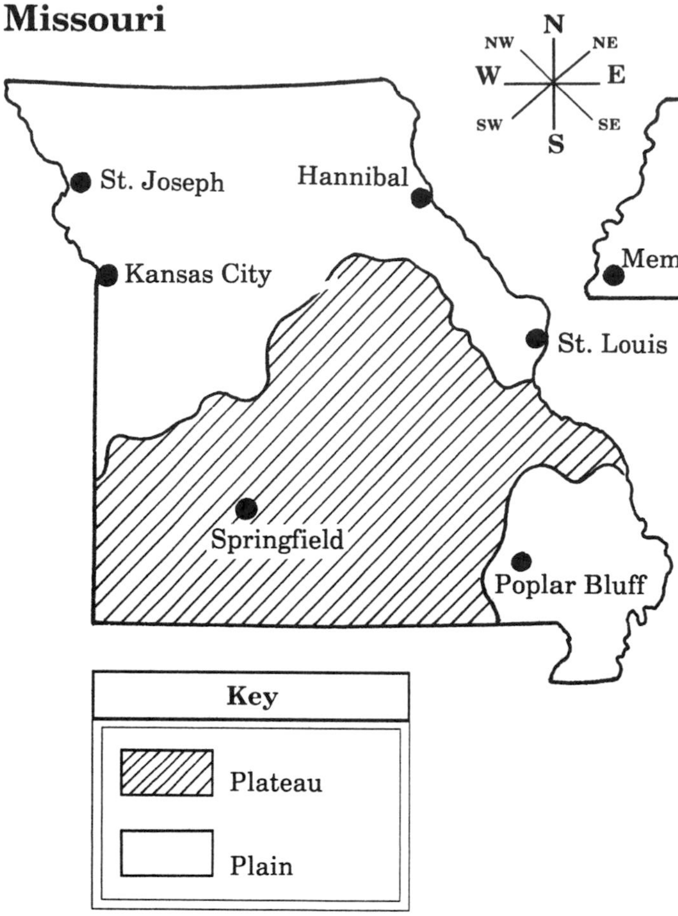

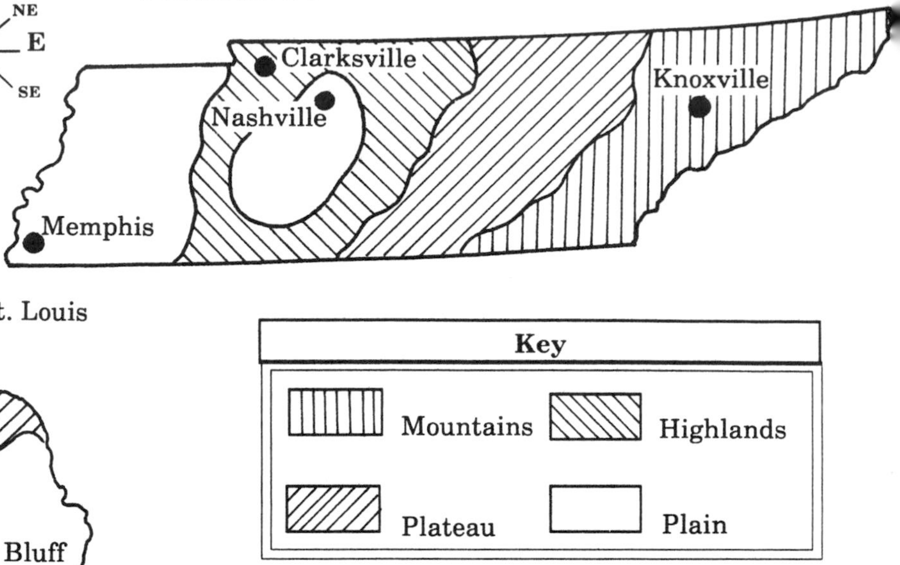

Key

Mountains	Highlands
Plateau	Plain

Key

Plateau
Plain

1. The southeastern corner of Missouri is a _____ .
2. The northern part of Missouri is a _____ .
3. Most of southern Missouri is a _____ .
4. What type of land is between Kansas City and Hannibal?_____
5. On a trip from St. Joseph to Poplar Bluff, what type of land will you travel over?

   _____

6. The eastern half of Tennessee is covered by_____ and a _____ .
7. Memphis is located on a _____ .
8. What two features do Tennessee and Missouri share?_____
   and _____
9. The central part of Tennessee is mostly _____ .
10. What types of land will you cross between Memphis and Knoxville? _____

    _____

11. The northeastern part of Tennessee has _____ .
12. Which of the states is almost half plateau? _____

Types of Land

Name _____

Use this map of the United States and a large wall map to answer the questions.

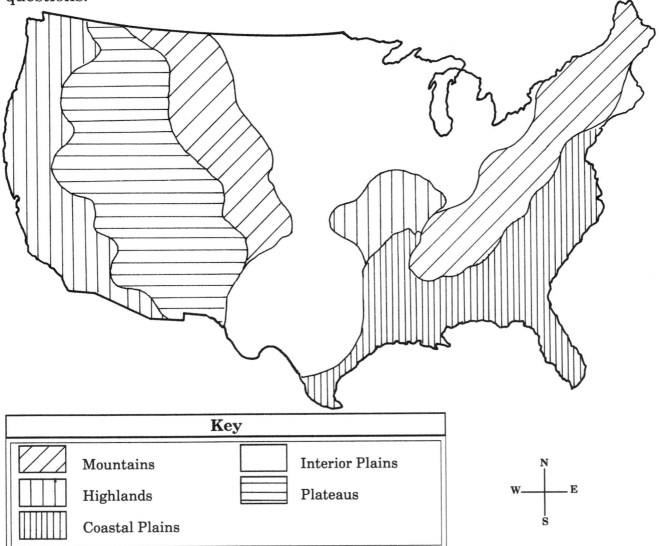

Key		
Mountains		Interior Plains
Highlands		Plateaus
Coastal Plains		

N
W——E
S

1. The western coast of the United States is composed of _____ .
2. The central part of the United States is _____ .
3. The northeastern part of the United States has _____ .
4. What does the symbol ⬚ stand for on the map? _____
5. In which part of the United States will you find coastal plains? _____
6. The state of California is mostly _____ .
7. Florida is composed of _____ .
8. The southern part of Texas is a _____ .
9. What symbol is used to show mountains? _____

Alaska and New York

Name —————————————————

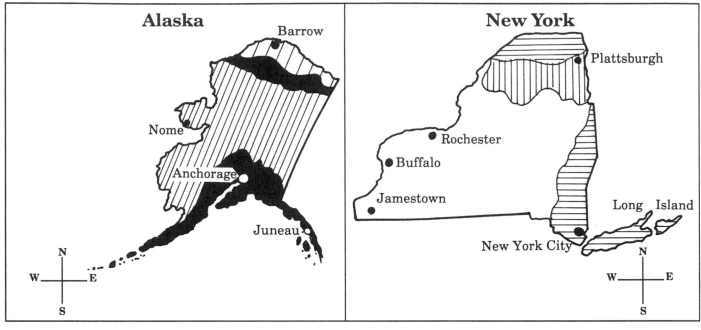

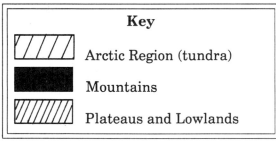

Key

▨ Arctic Region (tundra)

■ Mountains

▨ Plateaus and Lowlands

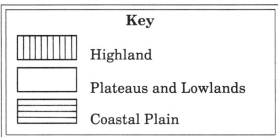

Key

▥ Highland

☐ Plateaus and Lowlands

▤ Coastal Plain

1. Barrow is part of the ————————————— Region.
2. Most of Alaska is covered with ————————————————— .
3. The southern part of Alaska is ————————————————— .
4. What type of land would you travel over from Barrow to Juneau? ——————
   ————————————————————————————— .
5. The northeastern part of New York is mostly ————————————— .
6. Both New York and Alaska have ————————————— and lowlands.
7. Plattsburgh, New York, is located in which part of the state – southwest or
   northeast?—————————————————
8. The western half of New York is composed of ————————————— .
9. The extreme northern part of New York is a ————————————— .
10. Is Nome on the eastern or western coast of Alaska? —————————————
11. Name the city on the map of Alaska which is farthest to the east. ——————
12. If you travel straight south from Plattsburgh to New York City, what types of
    land will you cross? —————————————————————————

Physical Features of the United States

Name _____

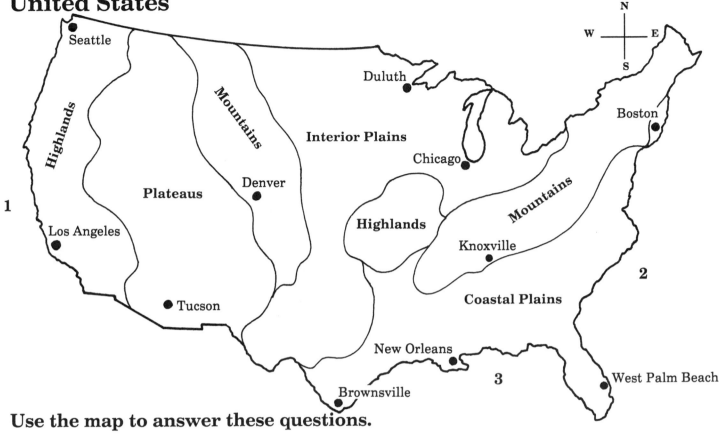

Use the map to answer these questions.

1. Name the two cities on the map found in mountain areas.

   _____   _____

2. Name the three cities found on coastal plains.

   _____   _____   _____

3. Seattle and Los Angeles are found on which coast – east or west? _____

4. Name the two cities located on the interior plains. _____

5. Your home state is located on which type of land? _____

Use a map of North America and the map above to answer these questions.

1. Identify the bodies of water marked with numbers on the map above.

   (1) _____   (2) _____   (3) _____

2. The mountains on the eastern side of the United States are the

   _____ .

3. The _____ Mountains are in the western part of the United States.

4. Is Boston on the eastern or western coast of the United States? _____

Political Maps

Concept: Political maps show the boundaries between countries.

Objective: To demonstrate how political maps show boundaries between countries.

Vocabulary: political, boundary, border, international, continent, country, territory

Background Information:
- Political maps show boundaries, or borders, and usually show the capital city of each country, state, etc. Political maps may also give other detailed information about cities, roads, rivers, and lakes.
- International borders are those agreed to by people.
- Some borders follow natural features but most are plotted by surveyors. When a river or mountain forms a border, each country gets one half of it.
- Other borders were settled by treaties between countries. Many European countries saw their borders change after World War I and/or II.

Teaching Suggestions

1. Students are most familiar with political maps because people use political maps to find the locations of cities and countries. Symbols on a political map tell where exact cities or countries are located. Many of today's maps are a combination of physical and political maps. Use a large wall map of North America to introduce the students to political boundaries. Point out the borders between the countries of Canada, the United States, and Mexico. A large map of the United States will show the borders between states. The activity page *What Is a Political Map?* utilizes a map of the midwestern United States.

2. The activity page *Counties in Arizona* shows the county boundaries and each county seat. You should explain the purpose of a county and its seat. Dividing a state into these smaller units of government called counties helps people to take better care of local legal matters. Marriage licenses, death certificates, deeds to property, etc., are all taken care of at the local level. Without these smaller divisions, all legal matters would require a trip to the state capital.

3. Before doing the activity page *Learning about Australia,* explain that Australia is the only continent which is also a country. Australia is divided into six states and two mainland territories. Explain to the students how a territory differs from a state. A territory is a part of a nation which is not accorded statehood or provincial status. One of the territories, the Australian Capital Territory, is similar in status to the District of Columbia in the U.S.

4. An interesting fact to share with the students before beginning the activity page *Countries and Cities in South America* is that all South American countries are Spanish-speaking except one. The exception is Brazil, whose people speak Portuguese.

5. The activity page *Northwestern Africa* may be a bit difficult since many of these place names will be unfamiliar to the students. Many of the countries of Africa have become independent and changed their names since World War II. Show the class a large wall map of the world. This will help them see how large Africa truly is.

Additional Activities

1. One of the quickest ways to show students how boundaries change is with the use of historical maps. If you don't have any, maybe you could borrow some from a junior high or high school history teacher. One example of drastic change is Poland because it did not exist in 1914. A map of Europe in the 1930's will show a large country labeled Poland. After World War II, Poland is still in existence, but smaller.

2. Using historical maps of North America, let the students see how the United States has changed.

3. Have the students ask their parents or grandparents to tell them why Libya has been in the news so often in the last ten years. Their grandparents might be able to also give students information about northern Africa and the battles fought there during World War II.

What Is a Political Map?   Name _____

Midwestern United States

1. What do these three symbols stand for on this map?

   A. ★ _____

   B. ● _____

   C. - - - - _____

2. The _____ forms the boundary between Missouri and Illinois.

3. _____ forms the boundary between Wisconsin and Michigan.

4. The eastern boundary of North Dakota is formed by the _____.

5. Ohio's western boundary is formed by the state of _____.

6. The southern part of Iowa is bordered by the state of _____.

7. What are the capital cities of these states?

   A. Kansas _____   D. North Dakota _____

   B. Indiana _____   E. Michigan _____

   C. Wisconsin _____   F. Illinois _____

8. The _____ River is north of Indianapolis.

9. Name the four lakes shown on this map. _____

   _____

10. Name the river which cuts South Dakota in half. _____

11. The northeastern border of Michigan is formed by Lake _____.

12. Chicago is on the coast of Lake _____.

Counties in Arizona

Name _____

Arizona County Map

Legend	
county seats	★
county lines	——

1. What do these symbols stand for on the map?

A. _____

B. — _____

2. What county is located in the southwest corner of the state?_____

3. Is Pima in the northern or southern part of Arizona?_____

4. Name the county seat for each county listed.

   A. Cochise _____   D. Yuma _____

   B. Mohave _____   E. Coconino _____

   C. Greenlee _____   F. Navajo _____

5. Is Cochise east or west of Pima County? _____

6. The county directly north of Yuma is _____.

7. What is the county seat for Santa Cruz? _____.

8. Name the county which is south of Graham. _____

9. What is the smallest county in Arizona? _____

10. Name the river which flows through Yuma. _____

11. The county seat of Pinal is _____.

12. Which county and county seat have the same name? _____

Learning about Australia

Name _____

Use this map of Australia to answer the questions.

Cape York Peninsula

Cooktown
Townsville
Darwin
Northern Territory
INDIAN OCEAN
La Grange
Alice Springs
Queensland
Rockhampton
Great Sandy Desert
Birdsville
Brisbane
PACIFIC OCEAN
Western Australia
South Australia
Eucla
New South Wales
Perth
Canberra
Newcastle
Sydney
Australian Capital Territory
Adelaide
Victoria
Melbourne
Tasmania
Hobart

N
W — E
S

Legend			
★ national capital	▲ state capital	● city	--- state boundary

1. Name the six states and two territories shown on this map of Australia.

   _____

   _____

2. What is the national capital of Australia? _____
3. Name the northern-most city on this map. _____
4. The _____ Ocean is east of Australia.
5. Alice Springs is in _____ .
6. The _____ Desert is in Western Australia.
7. _____ Peninsula forms the northern part of Queensland.
8. Is Eucla in the southeastern or southwestern part of West Australia? _____
9. The _____ Ocean is west of Australia.
10. Newcastle is in the state of _____ .
11. Cooktown is in the state of _____ .
12. Name the state directly north of Victoria. _____
13. Which of Australia's states is an island? _____

Countries and Cities in South America

Name _____

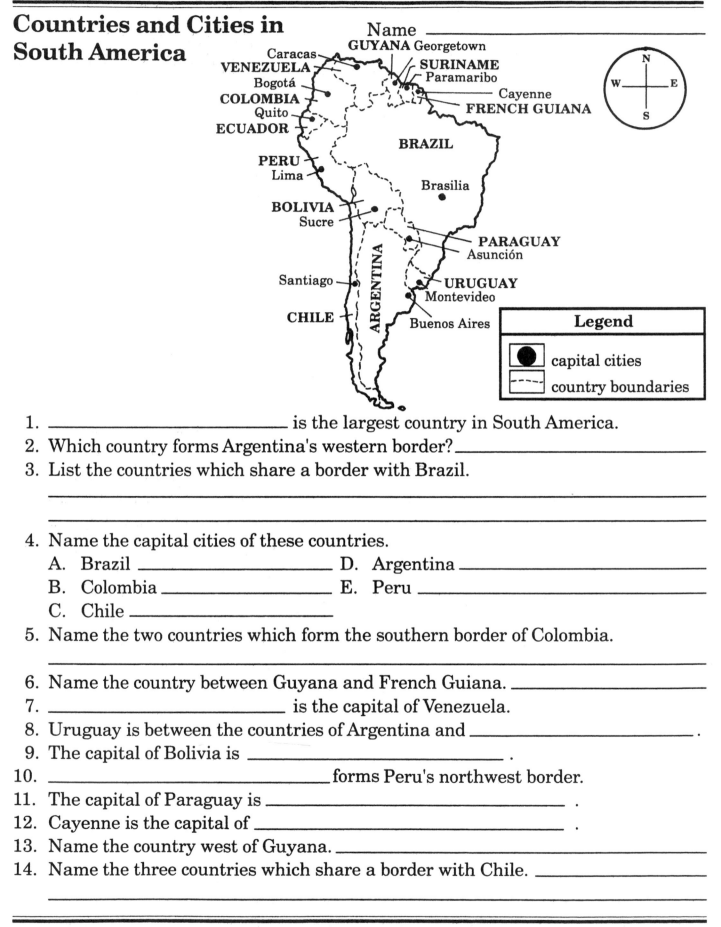

1. _____ is the largest country in South America.
2. Which country forms Argentina's western border? _____
3. List the countries which share a border with Brazil.

   _____

   _____

4. Name the capital cities of these countries.
   A. Brazil _____ D. Argentina _____
   B. Colombia _____ E. Peru _____
   C. Chile _____
5. Name the two countries which form the southern border of Colombia.

   _____

6. Name the country between Guyana and French Guiana. _____
7. _____ is the capital of Venezuela.
8. Uruguay is between the countries of Argentina and _____ .
9. The capital of Bolivia is _____ .
10. _____ forms Peru's northwest border.
11. The capital of Paraguay is _____ .
12. Cayenne is the capital of _____ .
13. Name the country west of Guyana. _____
14. Name the three countries which share a border with Chile. _____

   _____

Northwestern Africa

Name _____

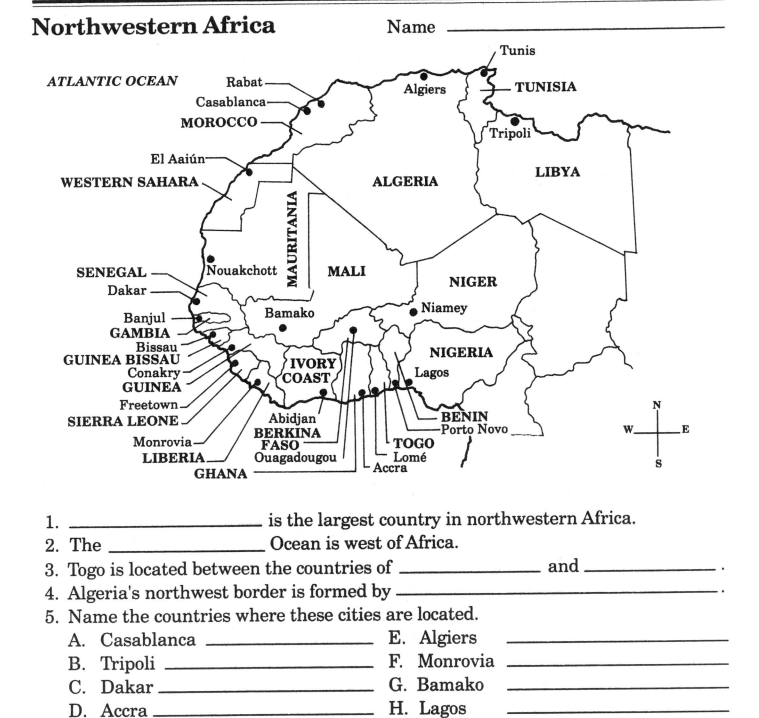

1. _____ is the largest country in northwestern Africa.
2. The _____ Ocean is west of Africa.
3. Togo is located between the countries of _____ and _____ .
4. Algeria's northwest border is formed by _____ .
5. Name the countries where these cities are located.

    A. Casablanca _____   E. Algiers _____

    B. Tripoli _____   F. Monrovia _____

    C. Dakar _____   G. Bamako _____

    D. Accra _____   H. Lagos _____

6. Libya is east of the country of _____ .
7. Benin is located between Nigeria and _____ .
8. Lomé is in the country of _____ .
9. Is Mali east or west of Mauritania? _____
10. Abidjan is in _____ .
11. Is Gambia north or south of Mauritania? _____
12. Niamey is in the southwestern corner of _____ .

Thematic Maps

Concept: Cartographers use thematic maps to show particular features of the physical or political environment.

Objective: To show how thematic maps tell about a particular topic, such as rainfall.

Vocabulary: thematic, environment, climate, population, revenue

Background Information:
- Thematic maps are drawn by cartographers to show specific information about a place. These maps may focus on a single topic, such as crops, climate, population, wildlife, minerals, or history. Thematic maps may also cover any specific area, such as a continent, a country, a state, a city, etc.
- Often a state will produce a thematic map to show major tourist attractions located within its borders.
- Thematic maps can focus on any given topic.

Teaching Suggestions

1. The activity pages are designed to expose students to a variety of themes while requiring the use of the many skills taught earlier in this book. They will need to use the compass rose to complete the first activity page *Products in California.*

2. The activity page *Where Is It Raining?* shows a precipitation map of South America. Students will compare the precipitation map to the political map of the continent.

3. The map on activity page *Tilling the Soil* shows the crop that the majority of acres are used for in a particular area. For instance, cotton is not the only crop grown in the southern states, but more acres are used to grow cotton there than any other crop.

4. The average annual rainfalls of South Dakota and California are studied on the activity page *How Much Did It Rain?*

5. The population map on *What Is the Population?* shows an imaginary land. Students should understand that knowing an area's population is important. For example, people looking for places to begin businesses need to know the population of cities since it will affect the number of possible employees available as well as customers.

6. The activity page *Tourist Map of Oldtown* is an example of a tourist map used by various cities and regions of the country. Tourism has become an increasingly large source of revenue for many states, making these kind of thematic maps very popular. Tourists need a method for easily locating roads and attractions.

7. The activity page *How Much Revenue?* shows the amount of money produced by each product in a state. Addition and multiplication must be used to answer some of the questions.

Additional Activities

1. Make up a page similar to the activity page *Products in California* using your own state.

2. Several educational games are available which relate to this book, such as "20 Questions" educational card games. They are available at your local teachers' store.

Products in California

Name _____

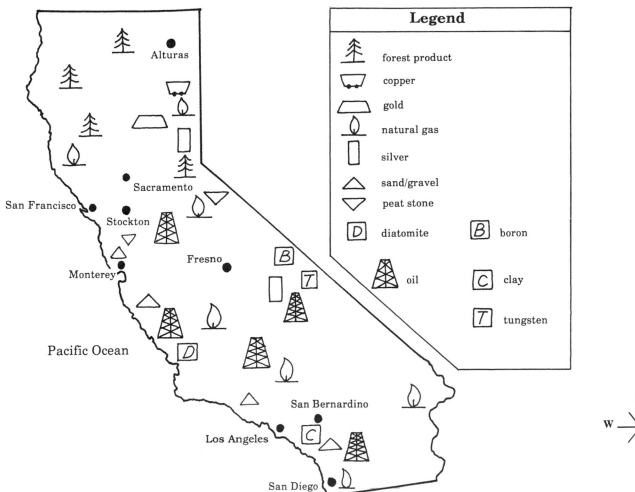

Legend

- 🌲 forest product
- copper
- gold
- natural gas
- silver
- △ sand/gravel
- ▽ peat stone
- [D] diatomite
- [B] boron
- oil
- [C] clay
- [T] tungsten

1. Northwestern California produces mostly _____ products.
2. Southeast of San Diego natural _____ is produced.
3. Southeast of Stockton _____ is drilled.
4. North of Fresno _____ is mined.
5. On the map, the city southwest of Sacramento is _____ .
6. Is Monterey east or west of Fresno? _____
7. Name four products found east of Fresno. _____
8. Is San Bernardino east or west of Los Angeles? _____
9. What is located west of California? _____
10. Is diatomite mined north or south of Los Angeles? _____
11. Is copper mined north or south of Alturas? _____
12. Is San Francisco north or south of Monterey? _____
13. Does California mine any gold near San Diego? _____
14. Is San Bernardino north or south of San Diego? _____

Where Is It Raining?

Name _____

Use both maps to answer these questions about South America.

South America – Precipitation Map

South America – Political Map

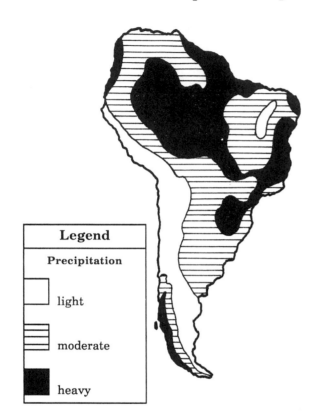

Legend

Precipitation

☐ light

▤ moderate

■ heavy

1. What do these symbols stand for on the precipitation map?

   ☐ A. _____   ▤ B. _____   ■ C. _____

2. The lightest precipitation falls mainly on the _____ part of South America.

3. The heaviest precipitation falls mainly in the _____ part of South America.

4. The majority of Argentina receives _____ precipitation.

5. The majority of South America receives _____ precipitation.

6. Most of Chile receives _____ precipitation.

7. The northwestern tip of Colombia receives _____ precipitation.

8. Does the southern half of Chile or the southern half of Argentina receive more precipitation? _____

9. The western half of Ecuador receives _____ precipitation.

10. Most of Brazil receives _____ precipitation.

Tilling the Soil

Name _____

Use this map to answer the questions on page 86.

Agriculture Map

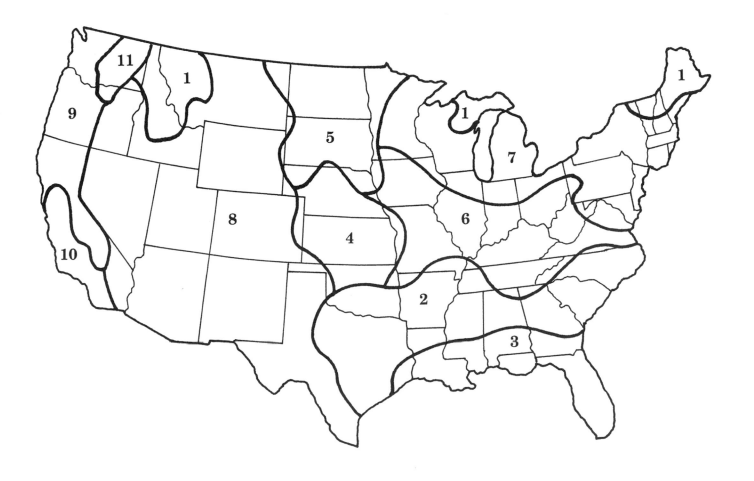

Legend		
1. Timber	5. Spring wheat	9. Pacific hay, pasture, and timber
2. Cotton	6. Corn and livestock	10. Pacific fruits and vegetables
3. Subtropical fruits, vegetables	7. Dairy, hardy crops	11. Wheat
4. Winter wheat	8. Livestock ranching	

Tilling the Soil (Continued)   Name _____

Use the map on page 85 to answer these questions.

1. The northeastern corner of the United State has _____ .
2. What types of crops are found on the Pacific coast?

   _____   _____

3. What is a common crop grown in many southern states? _____
4. What two types of wheat are grown in 4 and 5? _____

   _____

5. Much of the land in the western part of the United States is used for _____

   _____

6. What is most of the land in your state used for? _____

   _____

Use the map on page 85 and a political map of the United States to help you answer these questions.

1. What crops are grown in Florida? _____

   _____

2. Name the states where cotton is a major crop. _____

   _____

   _____

3. The major crop in Kansas is _____ .
4. The eastern part of Washington grows _____ .
5. Southwestern California grows _____ .
6. North and South Dakota are major producers of _____ .
7. Which of these states is a major producer of corn – Maine, Illinois, or California?

   _____

8. What is done in western Texas? _____
9. Michigan and Wisconsin produce _____ .
10. The northern half of Idaho produces _____ products and hay.
11. Most of Nebraska produces winter _____ .
12. Hay, pasture, and timber are produced in _____ California.

How Much Did It Rain?

Name

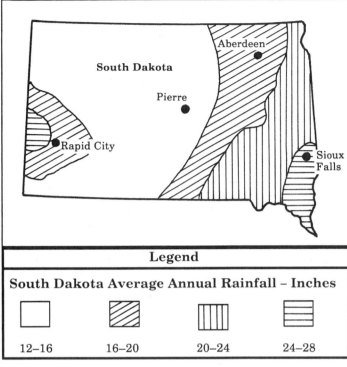

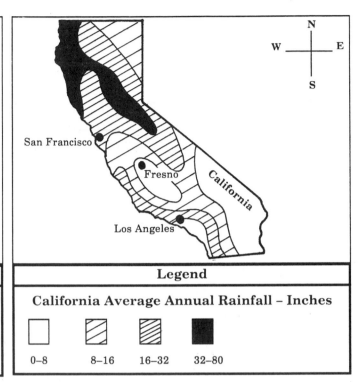

1. Aberdeen, South Dakota, receives between _____ inches of rain.
2. Which city receives more rain – Sioux Falls or Rapid City? _____
3. Northwestern South Dakota receives _____ inches of rain a year.
4. How much rain does Pierre, South Dakota, usually receive? _____
5. The southeastern corner of South Dakota receives _____ inches of rain.
6. What does the symbol ☐ mean on the map of California? _____
   _____
7. Southeastern California receives _____ inches of rain a year.
8. Los Angeles, California, receives an average of _____ inches of rain a year.
9. Which city receives more rain – Pierre, South Dakota, or San Francisco, California? _____
10. The northeastern part of California receives _____ inches of rain.
11. What does this symbol ■ mean on the map of California? _____
    _____
12. Does northern or southern California receive more rain? _____
13. Fresno, California, receives an average of _____ inches of rain.
14. Which city receives more rain – Sioux Falls, South Dakota, or Fresno, California? _____
15. The extreme northwestern corner of California receives _____ inches of rain a year.

What Is the Population?   Name _____

Use this map of an imaginary state to answer the following questions.

Population Map

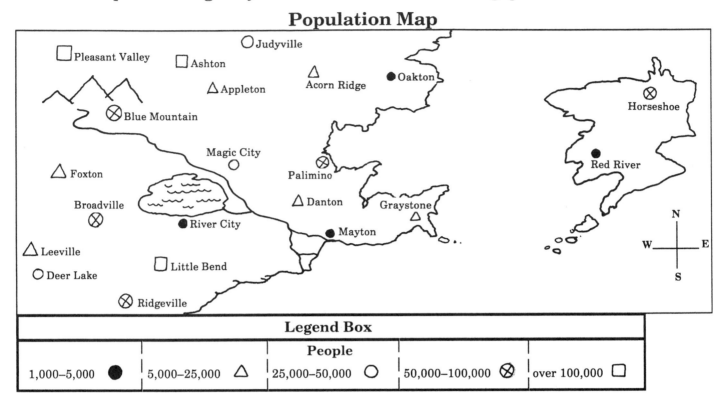

Legend Box				
People				
1,000–5,000 ●	5,000–25,000 △	25,000–50,000 ○	50,000–100,000 ⊗	over 100,000 ▢

1. Name the five cities with a population of 50,000 – 100,000.

   _____

2. Would you choose Foxton or Ashton for a baseball stadium which seats 50,000 people? _____

3. Name the three towns with a population over 100,000. _____

   _____

4. Which is bigger – Pleasant Valley or Mayton? _____

5. Which town has more people – River City or Magic City?_____

6. Which town has more people – Judyville or Danton? _____

7. Which is larger – Little Bend or Ridgeville? _____

8. Which city is smaller – Blue Mountain or Deer Lake? _____

9. How many towns have 1,000 – 5,000 people? _____

10. How many towns have 5,000 – 25,000 people? _____

11. Are there more people in Horseshoe or Red River? _____

12. Which city is smaller – Appleton or River City? _____

13. How many towns have 50,000 – 100,000 people?_____

14. Would you choose Deer Lake or Oakton for a stadium seating 10,000?_____

15. Which is larger – Graystone or Oakton?_____

Tourist Map of Oldtown

Name _____

Oldtown Tourist Map

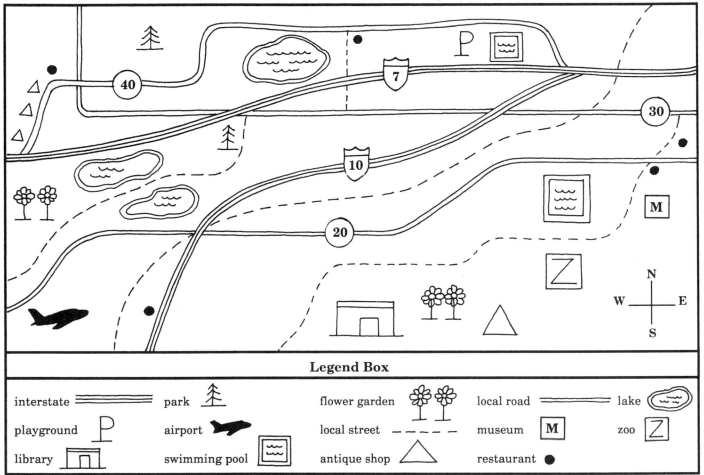

1. The airport is located between interstate _____ and local road _____ .
2. What attractions are north of interstate 7? _____

   _____
3. Could you take a local street from the airport to the library? _____
4. How many lakes are in Oldtown? _____
5. On which side of town is the museum located? _____
6. What is located at the point where local road 30 crosses interstate 7? _____
7. Name the road that runs north of the playground. _____
8. How many swimming pools are in Oldtown? _____
9. How many antique shops are in the town? _____
10. Is there a local street between the zoo and the swimming pool? _____
11. What is located north of local road 40? _____

   _____

How Much Revenue?

Name _____

Use the product map of this imaginary state to answer the questions.

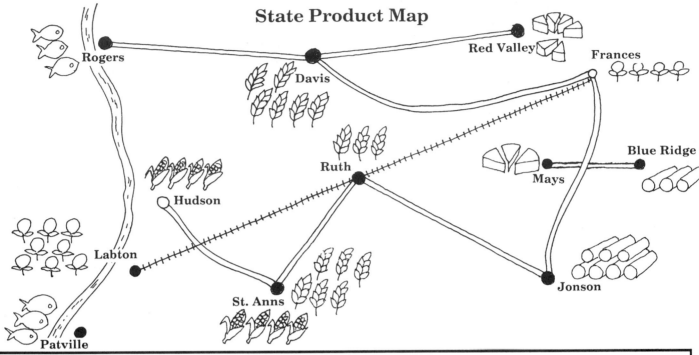

1. How much money, or revenue, does each symbol stand for?_____
2. How much does the state make from corn? _____
3. What product is grown near Jonson? _____
4. Does this state get more money from cotton or wood? _____
5. How much money does the state earn from fish? _____
6. Wheat is grown near the towns of _____
7. Patsville earns money by catching _____ .
8. The town of Red Valley produces _____ products.
9. What is the shortest way to transport cotton from Labton to Rogers?_____
10. How much money does the corn grown at Hudson produce for the state?_____
11. How much money does wheat produce for the state? _____
12. What is grown near Ruth? _____
13. How much revenue is produced in Ruth and Mays? _____

Glossary

Abstract – art that does not picture objects realistically

Abstract symbol – a picture on a map that is explained in the map's legend

Arctic – the region surrounding the North Pole

Arctic Circle – an imaginary line drawn parallel to and about 66° north of the equator

Bay – part of a sea or lake which reaches into land along a shore

Border – the line that separates one country, state, etc., from another; boundary

Boundary – see "Border"

Cape – land extending into the sea beyond the rest of the shoreline

Cardinal directions – the four main directions: north, south, east, and west

Cartographer – a person who draws or makes maps

Climate – the average of weather conditions in an area over several years

Coast – the land next to an ocean, sea, gulf, or lake

Compass – an instrument used to show direction

Compass Rose – a drawing on a map which shows directions

Contiguous – touching or in contact; *the 48 contiguous states*

Continent – a large area of land

Coordinates – a set of numbers that locate a place on the earth's surface

Country – a nation covering an area of land with specific boundaries

Degree – a unit to measure longitude and latitude

Delta – land at the mouth of a river made up of soil deposited by the river

Direction – the location of a point in relation to the North Pole

Distance – amount of space between points

Eastern Hemisphere – the half of the earth that includes Europe, Africa, Asia, and Australia

Elevation – height above sea level

Environment – the things, conditions, or influences around a particular place

Equator – an imaginary line around the center of the earth

Explorer – a person who goes into an area for the purpose of discovering new things

Globe – a tiny model of the earth; shaped like a sphere

Grid – a series of intersecting lines used to locate places

Hemisphere – the division of the earth into two equal parts; half a sphere

Highlands – an elevated, hilly or mountainous region

Horizontal – flat or level; parallel to the horizon

Interior – located inland from the coast

Intermediate directions – Northeast, Northwest, Southeast, or Southwest

International – between or among nations

Intersect – to cut across or through

Island – an area of land completely surrounded by water; not large enough to be called a continent

Isthmus – a narrow strip of land joining two large land areas

Junction – a place or point where things or lines meet

Key – a list of explanations for symbols; legend

Lake – a body of water completely surrounded by land; not as large as a sea or an ocean

Latitude – an imaginary set of lines which tells the location of points north and south of the equator

Legend – key explaining symbols found on a map

Location – position or place

Longitude – an imaginary series of lines which tells the location of points east or west of the prime meridian

Glossary (Continued)

Lowland – an area of low, flat land

Magnetic North Pole – a magnetic field which a north-seeking compass needle will point to; not precisely the geographical North Pole

Map – precisely drawn pictures of all or part of the earth

Maze – a complicated series of paths or passages

Meridian – an imaginary half circle on the earth's surface running from North Pole to South Pole; line of longitude

Mountain – high, rocky land usually with steep sides

Northern and Southern Hemispheres – the division of the earth into two equal parts north and south of the equator

North Pole – the northern end of the earth's axis

Ocean – a large body of salt water covering about three-fourths of the earth's surface; Atlantic, Pacific, Indian, Arctic, and Antarctic

Pampas – the vast grassy plains of South America, especially of Argentina

Parallel – an imaginary line on the earth's surface parallel to the equator; line of latitude

Peninsula – land surrounded by water on three sides

Physical – of nature and all matter

Physical map – a map which shows the land and water features shaped by nature

Picture symbol – a drawing used on a map which looks like the item it stands for

Plain – a flat or gently rolling area

Plateau – broad, flat region, higher than its surroundings on at least one side

Political – to do with government, politics, etc.

Political map – a map which shows countries, states, capitals, and cities

Population – the number of persons living in a given area, such as a square mile

Prime Meridian – an imaginary line running from north to south, used to locate points east and west on the earth's surface

Relief – a method of drawing landforms on a map to give them a three-dimensional appearance

Revenue – the income (money) received from someone for something

River – a large stream of water which flows over land and empties into an ocean, lake, or another river

Satellite – a man-made object launched from the earth into space

Scale – a unit of measurement that stands for another unit of measurement

Sea – a large body of salt water mostly or wholly enclosed by land

Strait – a narrow waterway which connects two larger bodies of water

Survey – to find out measurements, boundaries, or elevation by measuring angles and distances

Symbol – a drawing that stands for a real thing

Terrain – natural features found on the earth's surface

Territory – a part of a nation that does not have statehood or provincial status

Thematic – relating to a subject or theme

Thematic map – a map which tells about a special topic, such as rainfall or population

Topography – the hills, mountains, plateaus, plains, or valleys making up an area of land

Tributary – a stream flowing into a larger stream or a river

Tundra – a vast, treeless plain in the arctic regions

Valley – lowland between hills or mountains

Vegetation – plant growth

Vertical – a straight line which runs up and down

Volcano – an opening in the earth that shoots out lava, rock, gases and ashes from time to time

Western Hemisphere – the half of the earth where North and South America are located

Answer Key

Not all activity pages are represented in the answer key.

Page 4
1. b. window
2. b. door
3. c. table
4. a. bed

5. c. window
6. c. door
7. a. table

1. *artwork*
2. *artwork*

3. *artwork*
4. *artwork*

1. desk
2. plant

3. dresser
4. one

Page 5
1. The Library
2. Robin Avenue

3. The Grocery Store
4. Spring Street

1. Spring Street
2. Danny's house

3. The Library
4. Acorn Road

1. – 6. *artwork required*

Page 7
1. S. America
2. Africa
3. Asia
4. N. America

5. Antarctica
6. Australia
7. Europe

A. Arctic
B. Pacific

C. Atlantic
D. Indian

1. – 7. *artwork required*

Page 8
1. Atlantic Ocean
2. Indian Ocean
3. Atlantic Ocean

4. Atlantic Ocean
5. land

1. North America
2. Indian Ocean
3. Arctic Ocean

4. Africa
5. Antarctica

1. – 7. *artwork required*

Page 10
1. Antarctica
2. Northern Hemisphere map
3. Western Hemisphere map
4. (will color North America red)
5. (will color Australia blue)

Page 11
Continents – Eastern Hemisphere
   Asia   Australia   Africa
   Antarctica   Europe
Continents – Western Hemisphere
   North America   South America
   Antarctica
Continents – Northern Hemisphere
   Asia   Africa   Europe
   N. America   South America
Continents – Southern Hemisphere
   South America   Australia
   Africa   Antarctica
Oceans – Eastern Hemisphere
  1. Arctic   2. Indian 3. Pacific
Oceans – Western Hemisphere
  1. Pacific   2. Arctic 3. Atlantic

Page 11 (continued)
Oceans – Northern Hemisphere
  1. Pacific   2. Atlantic 3. Arctic
Oceans – Southern Hemisphere
  1. Atlantic 2. Indian 3. Pacific

Page 13
7, 9, 11, 8, 12, 10, 5, 1, 3, 4, 6, 2

1. Rocky or Appalachian
2. Florida
3. Hawaii
4. Huron, Ontario, Michigan, Erie, Superior

Page 14
3, 4, 10, 12, 6, 2, 11, 7, 9, 1, 5, 8
1. – 6. *artwork required*

Page 17
1. Australia
2. Asia
3. Europe
4. North America

5. Africa
6. Antarctica
7. South America

A. Atlantic Ocean
B. Indian Ocean
C. Arctic Ocean
D. Pacific Ocean

E. Isthmus of Panama
F. Ural Mountains
G. Mediterranean Sea

artwork required for rest of page

Page 19
1. Mississippi, Florida, Tennessee, Georgia
2. New Hampshire
3. Nevada, Arizona, Oregon
4. New Mexico
5. – 7. *artwork required*

Page 21
T   7

Page 22
1. Redwood
2. Rose City
3. Redville
4. Parkwood
5. Eastwood

6. Beltville
7. Beltville
8. Eastwood
9. Parkwood
10. Acorn City

1. – 7. *artwork required*

Page 23
1. south
2. west
3. north

4. east

1. – 10. *artwork required*

Page 25
NW is northwest.
SW is southwest.
NE is northeast.
SE is southeast.

1. northwest
2. northeast
3. southeast
4. northeast
5. northeast

6. west
7. north
8. south
9. northeast

Page 26
1. west
2. northeast or southwest
3. northeast
4. southwest
5. west or southwest

6. south
7. northeast
8. south
9. east
10. west

11. east
12. northwest
13. east
14. southwest
15. southwest

Page 33
1. yes
2. 3
3. a parking lot
4. Summer Avenue
5. 4
6. south
7. Blue Street
8. 3

9. 6
10. 4
11. 2
12. Summer Ave.
13. a store and a parking lot
14. 12

Page 34
1. 0–500
2. over 100,000 people
3. D, J, B, C
4. 4
5. 500–1,000
6. I
7. J
8. N, F, K, U

9. 2
10. W, X, Z
11. (circle A, G, E, L)
12. (draw X on S, T, H, Y)

Page 35
1. Washington
2. 3
3. rice
4. Kansas, North Dakota
5. tobacco
6. timber
7. cotton
8. Pennsylvania, West Virginia

9. Iowa, Illinois, Indiana, Ohio **Nebraska**
10. timber, oranges/lemons
11. oranges/lemons
12. hay

Page 37
1. 10
2. 15
3. 30 feet
4. 10 feet
5. 50

6. 5 feet
7. 10 feet
8. 15 feet
9. – 10. *artwork required*

Page 38
1. 175 miles
2. 125 miles
3. 225 miles
4. Jessiville
5. 250 miles
6. Carville to Mayville is longer.
7. Jonville to Mayville is shorter.

Page 39
1. 15 miles
2. 15 miles
3. 6 miles
4. 9 miles
5. 36 miles

6. 24 miles
7. 12 miles
8. 15 miles
9. 36 miles
10. 12 miles

Page 40
1. 273
2. 10
3. 20 miles
4. local
5. 59 and 3
6. 60 miles
7. west
8. north
9. *artwork required*

Page 41
1. 800 miles
2. 1,000 miles
3. 600 miles
4. City I to city M is closer.
5. yes
6. no
7. 1,000 miles
8. west
9. east

Page 43
1. (A1) woods (C1) house
   (D4) factory (D1) swimming pool
   (B2) house (A3) library
2. C2, D1
3. A4, B2, B3, C1, C3
4. A1, B1, B4
5. house
6. swimming pool
7. one
8. two
9. woods
10. factory
11. – 13. *artwork required*

Page 44
1. D5
2. B1
3. C2
4. D3, D4
5. A2, B2, B3, C3
6. C4
7. B4, B5
8. Oakville
9. Sand, Red
10. Carlaville
11. – 15. *artwork required*

Page 45
1. *(will draw star)*
2. state boundaries
3. Miami
4. Nashville
5. D1
6. Raleigh
7. B4
8. Baton Rouge
9. B3
10. Oklahoma City
11. C1
12. Dallas
13. Atlanta, Montgomery
14. N. Carolina
15. Oklahoma, Arkansas, Louisiana
16. S. Carolina
17. Florida
18. Chattanooga
19. Raleigh, Charlotte

Page 47
1. B5
2. no
3. A3, A5, B3, D3, D5
4. Friendly Apple Island
5. yes
6. E2
7. Pirates' Island
8. D3, D5
9. no

Page 49
1. equator
2. 90
3. degrees
4. parallels of latitude
5. South Pole
6. 15°S
7. 45°S
8. 15°N
9. 90°S
10. Neither – they are the same distance.
11. 90°
12. above
13. N. America
14. 15° (N)
15. S. America
16. – 17. *artwork*

Page 51
1. 70 (°N)
2. 40°N
3. Brownsville, New Orleans, Miami
4. 40°N
5. San Francisco, Denver, St. Louis, Dallas, Memphis, Los Angeles, San Diego, Tallahassee
6. Atlantic
7. Mexico
8. north
9. Pacific
10. Canada
11. 50°N
12. Alaska
13. 30°N, 40°N
14. north
15. Seattle, Des Moines, Chicago, New York
16. 40°N
17. 40°N
18. yes
19. 30°N
20. Mexico

Page 52
1. south
2. 38°N
3. 42°N
4. 45°N
5. Boise, Idaho Falls, Pocatello
6. Roswell, New Mexico
7. Stockton, San Francisco, Fresno
8. 46°N and 48°N
9. Reno and Elko
10. 42°N
11. Washington, Oregon, Idaho, Montana

Page 53
1. Belgium, France, Spain, Portugal
2. 250 miles
3. 40°N
4. 50°N and 45°N
5. Belgium
6-12. *artwork required*

Page 55
1. north, south, east, west
2. prime meridian
3. east and west
4. North and South Poles
5. degrees
A. – D. *artwork required*

Page 56
1. 30°W
2. 15°E
3. 15°E and 30°E
4. 6
5. 0° – prime meridian
6. 15°E
7. 75°W
8. 15°E
9. 75°W
10. 30°E
11. 90°W
12. 30°E

Page 57
1. 73°W
2. Scranton, Philadelphia, Georgetown
3. 75°W
4. (Philadelphia) 75° W
   (Scranton) 76°W
   (Georgetown) 75°W
   (Newark) 74°W
5. Pennsylvania, New York, Connecticut, New Jersey, Delaware, Maryland, Virginia

Page 57 (continued)
6. 74°W and 75°W
7. 77°W
8. Harrisburg
9. 77°W
10. Canton

Page 58
1. 100°W
2. S. Dakota
3. Lisbon, N. Dakota
4. 104°W
5. north
6. Bowman, N. Dakota
7. 102°W
8. 96°W
9. North Dakota
10. 102°W
11. Pembina, Grafton, Grand Forks, Fargo, Lisbon
12. South Dakota

Page 59
1. *artwork required*
2. 10°E and 15°E
3. 10°W
4. 5°W and 10°W
5. prime meridian
6. 5°E and 15°E
7. Left of prime meridian – west; right of prime meridian – east
8. 20°E
9. east
10. Poland
11. east
12. Naples
13. west
14. 10°E
15. 5°E

Page 61
1. 0°
2. north
3. 10°S
4. north
5. Alaska
6. above
7. 10°N
8. west
9. 20°S
10. 70°W
11. 40°N
12. 60°W and 70°W
13. 100°W and 110°W
14. north
15. Brazil, Colombia, Ecuador

Page 62
Texas

Page 63
1. 20°N and 30°N
2. 150°E and 130°E
3. rocks
4. 140°E, 130°E, 120°E
5. cabin
6. Casey's Island
7. dock/Casey's Island
8. coast guard station, sharks, airplanes, sea gulls, rocks
9. Dark Island
10. 130°E, 120°E, 110°E, 100°E

Page 65
1. (41°N/112°W)
2. 32 1/2°N/111°W
3. 35 1/2°N/106°W
4. 40 1/2°N/107°W
5. 32 1/2°N/109 1/2°W
6. 39°N/105°W
7. 32 1/2°N/106 1/2°W
8. 35°N/106 1/2°W
9. 40°N/108°W
10. 37°N/113 1/2°W
(Students' coordinates should be close to these numbers.)

Page 65 (continued)

1. (Glenwood)
2. Salt Lake City
3. Delta
4. Nogales
5. Mexican Hat
6. Roosevelt
7. Truth or Consequences
8. Fillmore
9. Gallup
10. Superior

1. Arizona
2. Utah
3. New Mexico
4. (color Colorado yellow)

Page 66

1. (Atlanta)
2. Miami
3. Pittsburgh
4. Tulsa
5. San Jose
6. Phoenix
7. St. Louis
8. Billings
9. Milwaukee
10. Des Moines
11. Albany
12. Minneapolis
13. Dallas
14. Houston

Page 68

1. (52°N) (0°) (United Kingdom)
2. 44 1/2°N 20°E Yugoslavia
3. 52°N 21°E Poland
4. 59°N 18°E Sweden
5. 38°N 24°E Greece
6. 60°N 25°E Finland
7. 49°N 2°E France
8. 48°N 11°E Germany
9. 55°N 12°E Denmark
10. 60°N 10°E Norway
11. 56°N 5°W Scotland
12. 50°N 14°E Czech Republic
13. 47°N 7°E Switzerland
14. 53°N 10°E Germany
15. 51°N 13°E Germany
16. 53°N 6°W Ireland
17. 42°N 12°E Italy
18. 47°N 19°E Hungary
19. 48°N 16°E Austria
20. 52°N 5°E Netherlands

(Students' coordinates should be close to these numbers.)

Page 69

a diamond
a rectangle

Page 71

1. pampas
2. Andes
3. northern
4. Brazilian
5. pampas
6. Brazilian
7. Uruguay
8. Venezuela
9. Chile, Bolivia, Paraguay, Brazil, Uruguay
10. Uruguay

Page 72

1. plain
2. plain
3. plateau
4. plain
5. plateau and plain
6. mountains, plateau
7. plain
8. plateau, plain
9. highlands
10. plain, highlands, plateau, mountains
11. mountains
12. Missouri

Page 73

1. highlands
2. interior plains
3. mountains
4. plateaus
5. south
6. highlands
7. coastal plains
8. coastal plain
9. *artwork*

Page 74

1. Arctic
2. plateaus and lowlands
3. mountains
4. Arctic Region (tundra), plateaus and lowlands, mountains
5. highland and coastal plain
6. plateaus
7. northeast
8. plateaus and lowlands
9. coastal plain
10. western
11. Juneau
12. highland, plateau and lowlands, coastal plain

Page 75

1. Denver, Knoxville
2. Brownsville, New Orleans, West Palm Beach
3. west
4. Duluth, Chicago
5. (answers will vary)

1. (1) Pacific Ocean
   (2) Atlantic Ocean
   (3) Gulf of Mexico
2. Appalachian Mountains
3. Rocky
4. eastern

Page 77

1. A. capital cities
   B. cities
   C. state boundaries
2. Mississippi River
3. Lake Michigan
4. Red River
5. Indiana
6. Missouri
7. A. Topeka   D. Bismarck
   B. Indianapolis E. Lansing
   C. Madison   F. Springfield
8. Wabash
9. Superior, Michigan, Huron, Erie
10. Missouri River
11. Huron
12. Michigan

Page 78

1. A. county seats
   B. county lines
2. Yuma
3. southern
4. A. Bisbee   D. Yuma
   B. Kingman   E. Flagstaff
   C. Clifton   F. Holbrook
5. east
6. La Paz

Page 78 (continued)

7. Nogales
8. Cochise
9. Santa Cruz
10. Gila River
11. Florence
12. Yuma

Page 79

1. Western Australia, Queensland, New South Wales, Victoria, South Australia, Tasmania, Northern Territory, Australian Capital Territory
2. Canberra
3. Darwin
4. Pacific
5. Northern Territory
6. Great Sandy
7. Cape York
8. southeastern
9. Indian
10. New South Wales
11. Queensland
12. New South Wales
13. Tasmania

Page 80

1. Brazil
2. Chile
3. French Guiana, Suriname, Guyana, Venezuela, Colombia, Peru, Bolivia, Paraguay, Argentina, Uruguay
4. A. Brasilia   D. Buenos Aires
   B. Bogotá   E. Lima
   C. Santiago
5. Ecuador, Peru
6. Suriname
7. Caracas
8. Brazil
9. Sucre
10. Ecuador
11. Asunción
12. French Guiana
13. Venezuela
14. Peru, Bolivia, Argentina

Page 81

1. Algeria
2. Atlantic
3. Ghana, Benin
4. Morocco
5. A. Morocco   E. Algeria
   B. Libya   F. Liberia
   C. Senegal   G. Mali
   D. Ghana   H. Nigeria
6. Algeria
7. Togo
8. Togo
9. east
10. Ivory Coast
11. south
12. Niger

Page 83
1. forest
2. gas
3. oil
4. peat stone
5. San Francisco
6. west
7. boron, tungsten, oil, and silver
8. east
9. Pacific Ocean
10. north
11. south
12. north
13. no
14. north

Page 84
1. A. light
   B. moderate
   C. heavy
2. southwestern
3. northern
4. light
5. moderate
6. light
7. heavy
8. Chile
9. moderate
10. heavy

Page 86
1. timber
2. Pacific hay, pasture and timber, Pacific fruits and vegetables
3. cotton
4. winter and spring
5. livestock ranching
6. *answers will vary*

1. subtropical fruits and vegetables
2. N. Carolina, S. Carolina, Georgia, Alabama, Mississippi, Louisiana, Texas, Arkansas, Oklahoma, Tennessee
3. winter wheat
4. wheat
5. Pacific fruits and vegetables
6. spring wheat
7. Illinois
8. livestock ranching
9. dairy, hardy crops
10. timber
11. wheat
12. northern

Page 87
1. 16–20
2. Sioux Falls
3. 12–16
4. 12–16 inches
5. 24–28
6. 0–8 inches of rain a year
7. 0–8
8. 0–8
9. San Francisco
10. 8–16
11. 32–80 inches of rain a year
12. northern
13. 0–8
14. Sioux Falls
15. 32–80

Page 88
1. Horseshoe, Ridgeville, Broadville, Palimino, Blue Mountain
2. Ashton
3. Ashton, Pleasant Valley, Little Bend
4. Pleasant Valley
5. Magic City
6. Judyville
7. Little Bend
8. Deer Lake
9. 4
10. 6
11. Horseshoe
12. River City
13. 5
14. Deer Lake
15. Graystone

Page 89
1. 10, 20
2. 3 antique shops, 2 restaurants, park, lake, playground, swimming pool
3. no
4. 3
5. east
6. park
7. local road 40
8. 2
9. 4
10. yes
11. 3 antique shops, restaurant, park

Page 90
1. $5,000.00
2. $40,000.00
3. wood (trees)
4. cotton
5. $30,000.00
6. Davis, St. Anns, Ruth
7. fish
8. dairy
9. river
10. $20,000.00
11. $75,000.00
12. wheat
13. $30,000.00

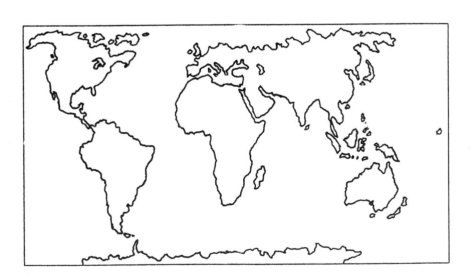